V

Sun Tzu's
Art of War
Playbook
Volume 5 of 9:

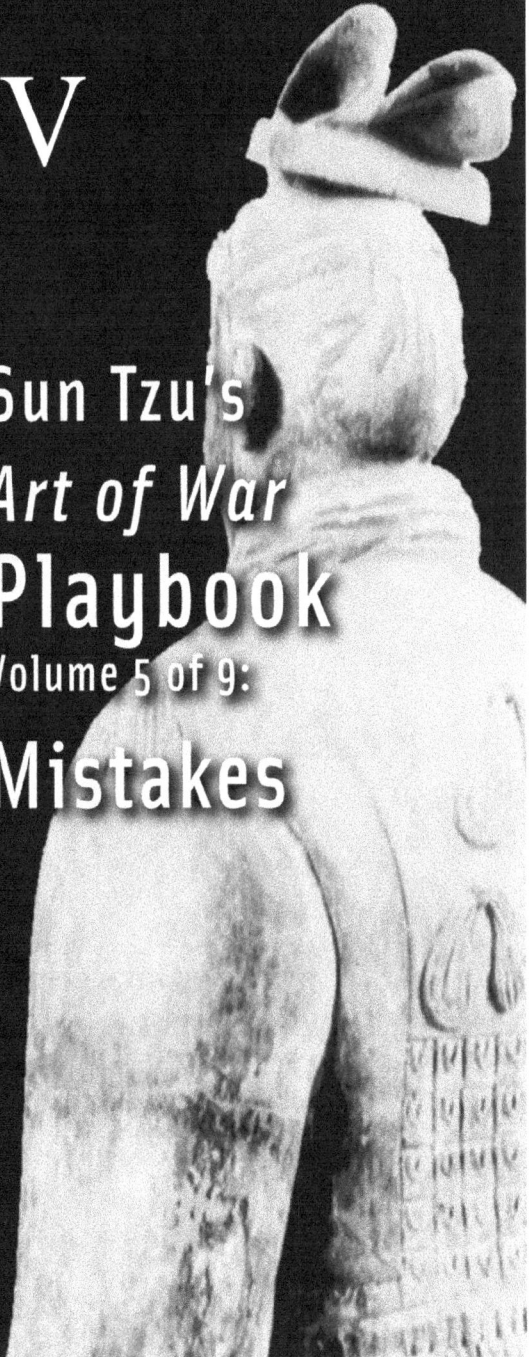

Mistakes

Gary
Gagliardi

Gary Gagliardi

Sun Tzu's Art of War Playbook

Volume Five: Mistakes

by Gary Gagliardi
The Science of Strategy Institute
Clearbridge Publishing

Published by
Science of Strategy Institute, Clearbridge Publishing
    suntzus.com   scienceofstrategy.org

First Print Edition
Library of Congress Control Number: 2014909969
Also sold as an ebook under the title Sun Tzu's Warrior Playbook
Copyright 2010, 2011, 2012, 2013, 2014 Gary Gagliardi
ISBN 978-1-929194-80-3 (13-digit) 1-929194-80-3 (10-digit)

Originally published as a series of articles on the Science of Strategy Website, scienceofstratregy.org. and
later as an ebook on various sites.

PO Box 33772, Seattle, WA 98133
Phone: (206)542-8947 Fax: (206)546-9756
beckyw@clearbridge.com
garyg@scienceofstrategy.org

Manufactured in the United States of America.
Interior and cover graphic design by Dana and Jeff Wincapaw.
Original Chinese calligraphy by Tsai Yung, Green Dragon Arts, www.greendragonarts.com.

Publisher's Cataloging-in-Publication Data
Sun-tzu, 6th cent. B.C.
Strategy , positioning, success, probability
    [Sun-tzu ping fa, English]
    Art of War Playbook / Sun Tzu and Gary Gagliardi.
    p.197 cm. 23
    Includes introduction to basic competitive philosophy of Sun Tzu

Clearbridge Publishing's books may be purchased for business, for any promotional use,
or for special sales.

Contents

Playbook Overview

Note: This overview is provided for those who have not read the previous volume of Sun Tzu's Art of War Playbook. *It provides an brief overview of the work in general and the general concepts framing the first volume.*

Sun Tzu's **The Art of War** is less a "book" in the modern Western sense than it is an outline for a course of study. Like Euclid's Geometry, simply reading the work teaches us very little. Sun Tzu wrote in in a tradition that expected each line and stanza to be studied in the context of previous statements to build up the foundation for understanding later statements.

To make this work easier for today's readers to understand, we developed the **Strategy Playbook**, the Science of Strategy Institute (SOSI) guidebook to explaining Sun Tzu's strategy in the more familiar format of a series of explanations with examples. These lessons are framed in the context of modern competition rather than ancient military warfare.

This Playbook is the culmination of over a decade of work breaking down Sun Tzu's principles into a series of step-by-step practical articles by the Institute's multiple award-winning author and founder, Gary Gagliardi. The original **Art of War** was written for military generals who understood the philosophical concepts of ancient China, which in itself is a practical hurdle that most modern readers cannot clear. Our **Art of War Playbook** is written for today's reader. It puts Sun Tzu's ideas into everyday, practical language.

The Playbook defines a new science of strategic competition aimed at today's challenges. This science of competition is designed as the complementary opposite of the management science that is taught in most business schools. This science starts, as Sun Tzu did himself, by defining a better, more complete vocabulary for discussing competitive situations. It connects the timeless ideas of Sun Tzu to today's latest thinking in business, mathematics, and psychology.

The entire Playbook consists of two hundred and thirty articles describing over two-thousand interconnected key methods. These articles are organized into nine different areas of strategic skill from understanding positioning to defending vulnerabilities. All together this makes up over a thousand pages of material.

Playbook Access

The Playbook's most up-to-date version is available as separate articles on our website. Live links make it easy to access the connections between various articles and concepts. If you become a SOSI Member, you can access any Playbook article at any time and access their links.

However, at the request of our customers, we also offer these articles as a series of nine eBooks. Each of the nine sections of the entire Playbook makes up a separate eBook, Playbook Parts One Through Nine. These parts flow logically through the Progress Cycle of listen-aim-move-claim (see illustration). Because of the dynamic nature of the on-line version, these eBooks are not going to be as current as the on-line version. You can see a outline of current Playbook articles here and, generally, the eBook version will contain most of the same material in the same order.

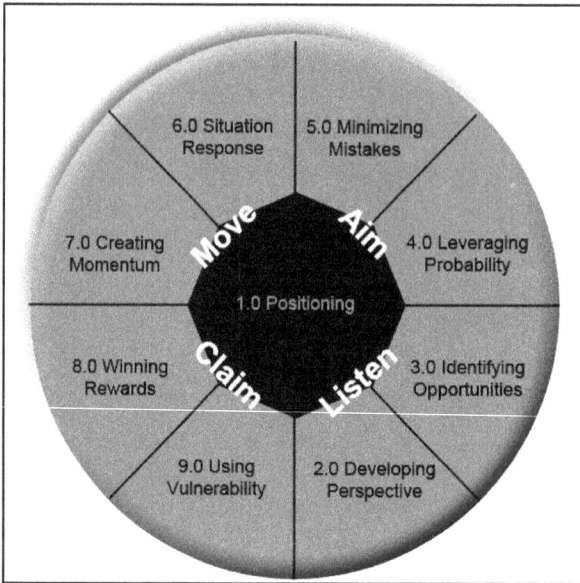

Nine categories of strategic skills define cycle that advances our positions:

1. Comparing Positions,

2. Developing Perspective,

3. Identifying Opportunities,

4. Leveraging Probability,

5. Minimizing Mistakes,

6. Responding To Situations,

7. Creating Momentum,

8. Winning Rewards, And

9. Defending Vulnerabilities.

Playbook Structure and Design

These articles are written in standard format including 1) the general principle, 2) the situation, 3) the opportunity, 4) the list of specific Art of War key methods breaking down the general principle into a series of actions, and 5) an illustration of the application of each of those key methods to a specific competitive situation. Key methods are written generically to apply to every competitive arena (business, personal life, career, sports, relationships, etc.) with each specific illustrations drawn from one of these areas.

A number identifies where each article appears in Playbook Structure. For example, the article 2.1.3 Strategic Deception is the third article in the first section of the second book in the nine volumes of the Strategy Playbook. In our on-line version, these links are live, clicking on them brings you to the article itself. We provide them because the interconnection of concepts is important in learning Sun Tzu's system.

Playbook Training

Training in Sun Tzu's warrior skills does not entail memorizing all these principles. Instead, these concepts are used to develop exercises and tools that allow trainees to put this ideas in practice. While each rule is useful, the heart of Sun Tzu system is the methods that connect all the principles together. Training in these principles is designed to develop a gut instinct for how Sun Tzu's strategy is used in different situations to produce success. Principles are interlinked because they describe a comprehensive conceptual mental model. Warrior Class training puts trainees in a situation where they must constantly make decisions, rewarding them for making decisions consist with winning productively instead of destructively.

About Positions

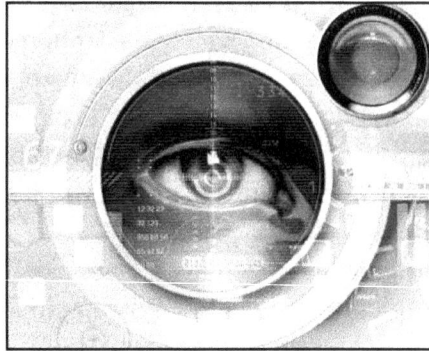

This first volume of Sun Tzu's Playbook focuses on teaching us the nature of strategic positions. "Position awareness" gives you a framework for understanding your strategic situation relative to the conditions around you. It enables you to see your position as part of a larger environment constructed of other positions and the raw elements that create positions. Master Sun Tzu's system of comparing positions, you can understand which aspect of your position are secure and which are the most dynamic and likely to change.

Traditional strategy defines a "position" as a comparison of situations. Game theory defines is as the current decision point that is arrive at as the sum or result of all previous decisions, both yours and those of others. Sun Tzu's methods of positioning awareness are different. They force you to see yourself in the eyes of others. Using these techniques, you broaden your perspective by gathering a range of viewpoints. In a limited sense, the scope of your position defines your area of control within your larger environment. In traditional strategy, five elements--mission, climate, ground, command, and methods--define the dimensions in which competitors can be compared.

Competition as Comparison

Sun Tzu saw that success is based on comparisons. This comparison must take place whenever a choice is made. For Sun Tzu, competition means a comparison of alternative choices or "positions". Battles are won by positioning before they are fought. These positions provide choices for everyone involved. Good positions discourage others from attacking you and invite them to support you. Sun Tzu's system teaches us how to systematically build up our positions to win success in the easiest way possible.

Competing positions are compared on the basis many elements, both objective and subjective. Sun Tzu's strategy is to identify these points of comparison and to understand how to leverage them. Learning Sun Tzu's strategy requires learning the details of how positions are compared and advanced. Sun Tzu taught that fighting to "sort things out" is a foolish way to find learn the strengths and weaknesses of a position. Conflict to tear down opposing positions is the most costly way to win competitive comparisons.

Today's More Competitive World

In the complex, chaotic world of today, we can easily get trapped into destructive rather than productive situations. Even our smallest decisions can have huge impact on our future. The problem is that we are trained for yesterday's world of workers, not today's world of warriors. We are trained in the linear thinking of planning in predictable, hierarchical world. This thinking applies less and less to today's networked, more competitive world.

Following a plan is the worker's skill of working in pre-defined functions in an internal, stable, controlled environment. The competitive strategy of Sun Tzu is the warrior's skill of making good decisions about conditions in complex, fast-changing, competitive environments. Sun Tzu's strategic system teaches us to adapt to the unexpected events that are becoming more and more common in our lives. We live in a world where fewer and fewer key events are planned. Navigating our new world of external challenges requires a different set of skills.

Most of us make our decisions without any understanding of competition. The result is that most of us lose as many battles as we win, never making consistent progress. Events buffet us, turning us in one direction and then the other. Too often, we end up repeating our past patterns of mistakes.

The Science of Strategy Institute teaches you the warrior's skills of adaptive response. There are many organizations that teach planning and organization. The Institute is one of the few places in the world you can get learn competitive thinking, and the only place in the world, with a comprehensive Playbook.

Seeing Situations Differently

Sun Tzu taught that a warrior's decision-making was a matter of reflex. As we develop our strategic decision-making skills, the critical conditions in situations simply "pop" out at us. This isn't magic. The latest research on how decisions are made tells us a lot about why Sun Tzu's principles work. It comes from using patterns to retrain our mind to see conditions differently. The study of successful response arose from military confrontations, where every battle clearly demonstrated how hard it is to predict events in the real world. Sun Tzu saw that winners were always those who knew how to respond appropriately to the dynamic nature of their situation.

Sun Tzu's principles provides a complete model for the key knowledge for understanding conditions in complex dynamic environments. This model "files" each piece of data into the appropriate place in the big picture. As the picture of your situation fills in, you can identify the opportunities hidden within your situation.

Making Decisions about Conditions

Instead of focusing on a series of planned steps, Sun Tzu's principles are about making decisions regarding conditions. It concerns itself with: 1) identifying the relative strengths and weaknesses of competitive positions, 2) advancing positions leveraging opportunities, and 3) the types of responses to specific challenges that work the most frequently. Using Sun Tzu's principles, we call these three areas position awareness , opportunity development , and situation response . Each area that we master broadens your capabilities.

- Position awareness trains us to recognize that competitive situations are defined by the relationship among alternative positions. Developing this perspective never ends. It deepens throughout our lives.
- Opportunity development explores the ground, testing our perceptions. Only testing the edges of perspective through action can we know what is true.
- S ituation response trains us to recognize the key characteristics of the immediate situation and to respond appropriately. Only by practice, can we learn to trust the viewpoint we have developed.

Success in competitive environments comes from making better decisions every day. Sharp strategic reflexes flow from a clear understanding of where and when you use which competitive tools methods.

The Key Viewpoints

As an individual, you have a unique and valuable viewpoint, but every viewpoint is inherently limited by its own position. The result is that people cannot get a useful perspective on their own situations and surrounding opportunities. The first formula of positioning awareness involve learning what information is relevant. The most advanced techniques teach how to gather that information and put it into a bigger picture.

Most people see their current situations as the sum of their past successes and failures. Too often people dwell on their mistakes while simultaneously sitting on their laurels. Sun Tzu's strategy forces you to see your position differently. How you arrived at your current position doesn't matter. Your position is what it is. It is shaped by history but history is not destiny.

In this framework, the only thing that matters is where you are going and how you are going to get there. As you begin to develop your strategic reflexes, you start to think more and more about how to secure your current position and advance it.

Seeing the Big Picture

Most people see all the details of their lives, but they cannot see what those detail mean in terms of the big picture. As you master position awareness, you don't see your life as a point but as a path. You see your position in terms of what is changing and what resources are available. You are more aware of your ability to make decisions and your skills in working with others.

Most importantly, this strategic system forces you to get in touch with your core set of goals and values.

Untrained people usually see their life in terms of absolutes: successes and failures, good luck and bad, weakness and strength. As you begin to master position awareness, you begin to see all comparisons of strength and weakness are temporary and relative. A position is not strong or weak in itself. Its strength or weakness depends on how it compares or "fits" with surrounding positions. Weakness and strength are not what a position is, but how you use it.

The Power of Perspective

Positional awareness gives you the specialized vocabulary you need to understanding how situations develop. Mastering this vocabulary, you begin to see the leverage points connecting past and future. You replace vague conceptions of "strength," "momentum," and "innovation" with much more pragmatic definitions that you can actually use on a day to day basis.

Mastering position awareness also changes your relationships with other people. It teaches you a different way of judging truth and character. This methods allow you to spot self-deception and dishonest in others. It also allows you to understand how you can best work with others to compensate for your different weaknesses.

Once you develop a good perspective of position, it naturally leads you to want to learn more about how you can improve you position through the various aspects of opportunity development covered in the subsequent parts of the Strategy Playbook.

Seeing the Invisible

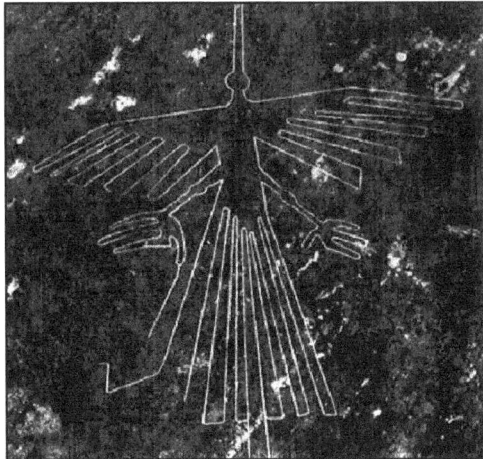

The "Nazca lines" are giant drawings etched across thirty miles of desert on Peru's southern coast. The patterns are only visible at a distance of hundreds of feet in the air. Below that, they look like strange paths or roads to nowhere. Just as we cannot see these lines without the proper perspective, people who master Sun Tzu's methods can <u>suddenly recognize situations</u> that were invisible to them before. Unless we have the right perspective, we cannot compare situations and positions successfully. The most recent scientific research explains why people cannot see these patterns for comparison without developing the network framework of adaptive thinking.[1]

Seeing Patterns

We can imagine patterns in chaotic situations, but seeing real pattern is the difference between success and failure. In our seminars, we demonstrate the power of seeing patterns in a number of exercises.

The <u>mental models</u> used by warrior give them "situation awareness." This situation awareness isn't just vague theory. Recent research shows that it can be measured in a variety of ways.[2] We now know that untrained people fall victim to a flow of confusing information because they don't know where its pieces fit. Those trained in Sun Tzu's mental models plug this stream of information quickly and easily into a bigger picture, transforming the skeleton's provided by Sun Tzu's system into a functioning awareness of your strategic position and its relation to other positions. Each piece of information has a place in that picture. As the information comes in, it fills in the picture, like pieces of a puzzle.

The ability to see the patterns in this bigger picture allows experts in strategy to see what is invisible to most people in a number of ways. They include:

- People trained in Art of War principles--<u>recognition-primed decision-making</u> --see patterns that others do not.
- Trained people can spot anomalies, things that should happen in the network of interactions but don't.
- Trained people are in touch with changes in the environment within appropriate time horizons.
- Trained people recognize complete patterns of interconnected elements under extreme time pressure.

Procedures Make Seeing Difficult

One of the most surprising discoveries from this research is that those who know procedures, that is, a linear view of events, alone have a ***more*** difficult time recognizing patterns than novices. An interesting study[3] examined the different recognition skills of three groups of people 1) experts, 2) novices, and 3) trainers who taught the standard procedures. The three groups were asked to pick out an expert from a group novices in a series of videos showing them performing a decision-making task, in this case, CPR. Experts were able to recognize the expert 90% of the time. Novices recognized the expert 50% of the time. The shocking fact was that trainers performed much worse that the novices, recognizing the expert only 30% of the time.

Why do those who know procedures fail to see what the experts usually see and even novices often see? Because, as research into <u>mental simulations</u> has shown, those with only a procedural model fit everything into that model and ignore elements that don't fit. In the above experiment, interviews with the trainers indicated that they assumed that the experts would always follow the procedural model. In real life, experts adapt to situations where unique conditions often trump procedure. Adapting to the situation rather than following set procedures is a central focus the form of strategy that the Institute teaches.

Missing Expected Elements

People trained to recognize the bigger picture beyond procedures also recognize when expected elements are missing from the picture. These anomalies or, what the cognition experts [4] describe as "negative cues" are invisible to novices *and* to those trained only in procedure. Without sense of the bigger pattern, people are focused too narrowly on the problem at hand. The "dog that didn't bark" from the Sherlock Holmes story, "Silver Blaze," is the most famous example of a negative cue. Only those working from a larger nonprocedural framework can expect certain things to happen and notice when they don't.

The ability to see what is missing also comes from the expectations generated by the mental model. Process-oriented models have the expectation of one step following another, but situation-recognition models create their expectations from signals in the environment. Research [5] into the time horizons of decision-makers shows that different time scales are at work. People at the highest level of organizations must look a year or two down the road, using strategic models that work in that timeframe, doing strategic planning. Decision-makers on the front-lines, however, have to react within minutes or even seconds to changes in their situation, working from their strategic reflexes. The biggest danger is that people get so wrapped up in a process that they lose contact with their environment.

Decisions Under Pressure

Extreme time pressure is what distinguishes front-line decision-making from strategic planners. One of the biggest discoveries in cognitive research [6] is that trained people do much better in seeing their situation instantly and making the correct decisions under time pressure. Researchers found virtually no difference between the decisions that experts made under time pressure when comparing them to decisions made without time pressure. That research also finds that those with less experience and training made dramatically worse decisions when they were put under time pressure.

The central argument for training our strategic reflexes is that our situation results, not from chance or luck, but from the instant decisions that that we all make every day. Our position is the sum of these decisions. If we cannot make the right decisions on the spot, when they are needed, our plans usually come to nothing. This is why we describe training people's strategic reflexes as helping them "do at first what most people only do at last."

The success people experience seeing what is invisible to others is dramatic. To learn more about how the strategic reflexes we teach differ from what can be planned, read about the contrast between planning and reflexes here . As our many members report, the success Sun Tzu's system makes possible is remarkable.

1 Chi, Glaser, & Farr, 1988, The Nature of Expertise, Erlbaum
2 Endsley & Garland, Analysis and Measurement of Situation Awareness
3 Klein & Klein, 1981, "Perceptual/Cognitive Analysis of proficient CPR Performance", Midwestern Psychological Association Meeting, Chicago.
4 Dr. David Noble, Evidence Based Research, Inc.In Gary Klein, Sources of Power, 1999
5 Jacobs & Jaques, 1991, "Executive Leadership".In Gal & Mangelsdofs (eds.), Handbook of Military Psychology, Wiley
6 Calder, Klein, Crandall,1988, "Time Pressure, Skill, and Move Quality in Chess". American Journal of Psychology, 101:481-493

About Minimizing Mistakes

In Volume Five, Sun Tzu's Plabooks explains the safest way to explore an opening as an opportunity for advancing a position. Though we learn more from our mistakes than our successes, we must design new ventures so any mistakes don't damage our current position.

All new ventures fail if we pursue them with half measures. However, even if we pursue new ventures wholeheartedly, many will still fail. How do we make sure that those failures don't damage our position? We need the principles for minimizing mistakes to test our ideas. They minimize our risk and the impact of our failures. They also dramatically increases the eventual certainty of success.

The Limits of Planning

Successful competition requires knowing what you can control and what you cannot control. To improve your position, each move must return more than it costs. If you knew which new move were going to be profitable, there would be no need for this set of principles. The truth is that you cannot know how valuable a new position will be before you win it. Therefore, you control what you can, which are the costs.

Competitive environments are dynamic. Within them, people's plans collide continually, creating situations that no one planned. You cannot predict competitive conditions. This limits traditional planning. The longer you try to perfect your plans by gathering more and more information, the more expensive your new move becomes and the more likely it is that the opportunity will pass you by. When you plan, you make decisions in advance. However, in dynamic competitive arenas, it is usually less costly and much safer to test a position in a small way to see what happens and then adapt to the conditions you discover.

Instead of planning, Sun Tzu's Playbooks teaches us to think about testing. You want to get a new venture off the ground as soon as possible. Inertia destroys enthusiasm for any new project. Planning long, careful, drawn-out campaigns drains your limited resources. These campaigns are more likely to fail. Bigger experiments are never better experiments.

People think that the more detailed the plan, the safer a new venture is. This is true in controlled environments, but the opposite is true in any competitive arena. Planning is meaningless without testing your plans. The desire to keep planning creates sluggish organizations. The longer you plan, the more effort you invest. While you are planning, your competitors can test their ideas to see what works. It doesn't matter how smart you think you are. You can't get ahead by falling behind your competitors.

You can sometimes go into a new position too quickly, but you can never start testing too soon. You can continue to plan or your can start testing your venture to see what happens. You can't do both at once.

Do Less, Not More

The goal of all of Sun Tzu's Playbook is to improve your competitive position. In this volume, we learn the power of doing less, not more. When you see an appealing opportunity, you naturally want to pursue it. But your time and efforts are limited. You cannot always do more. You must grow by subtraction. If a new opportunity makes sense, it expands on what you are currently doing. This means that you must decrease what you are doing elsewhere. A decision to do more must be coupled with a decision to do less.

Let me give you an example from my personal experience of how to grow a business by making it simpler.

When we started our software company, we started as general consultants. Our most profitable jobs came from database development, so we slowly stopped doing other projects. By focusing on database projects, our business doubled. Then our most profitable projects were accounting related, so we focused on those projects. We again doubled in size. Then the most profitable accounting sales came from resellers. So we stopped other sales and doubled again. Then the most profitable sales were from large systems. We stopped selling smaller systems. We doubled again. The we saw that our most profitable sales came from order processing. We stopped selling other types of accounting software and doubled in size again.

We became one of the Inc. 500 fastest-growing companies in America not by doing more and more, but by doing less and less. And we did it without any outside financing or borrowing money because we were always working at what was most profitable.

You use every opportunity to further refine and simplify your focus. A focused venture is successful. An unfocused venture fails. Doing one thing better and better is easy. Doing more and more things well is hard. A concentrated effort is powerful. A divided effort is weak. Well-defined positions make you successful. A confused position is costly. Clear-cut goals keep you on track. Confused goals get you nowhere.

The more focused your efforts are, the easier it will be to win competitive comparisons. Still, the best way to win competitive comparison isn't constantly being compared to others. Success comes from avoiding competitive battles. You want to develop positions that stand out from the crowd, that are unique. You win by avoiding comparison.

This is the power of focus.

The Goal is to Win Rewards

The proof of any new positions is getting rewarded for controlling it. You must avoid positions in which the rewards are poorly defined. You must avoid positions in which you are not sure who will reward you for that position. You must avoid ventures in which it isn't clear how you will make money selling your product.

Instead, these principles teach us to choose opportunities where it is easy to know who rewards you for having that position and why. What is the easiest way of assuring that a position's value? Go after positions similar to those that are already being rewarded. In business, these means you concentrate your efforts on the most profitable areas of commerce. Reward your early customers for trusting you. Advertise and promote your success with early adopters. Choose markets that generate repeat business to avoid high sales and marketing costs.

Internal Distractions

You want to improve your position. You are going to be devoting time and resources to improving it. Those resources are taken from elsewhere. Sun Tzu tells us that people are naturally frightened by change. A new venture is always a threat to more established parts of a position, especially when we work within a larger organization.

Internal conflict and political divisions over what is "fair" can undermine your success in several different ways. Ignorant of the need and nature of real opportunities, people in more established part of an organization want to force expansion on their schedule. Ignorant of the dynamic nature of competition, they want to abandon new ventures when they get difficult. Sun Tzu calls this hamstringing the army.

The confusion between controlled and dynamic environments underlies the conflict between an established enterprise and every new venture. An established enterprise exists in a more controlled and predictable space than a new venture. Existing organizations want to plan new ventures like they do proven operations. They think they can manage a new venture according to the same principles that they use to manage established businesses. The goal of a new enterprise isn't to be predictable but to find some way to survive.

New ventures require different priorities and are run by different sets of principles. The demands of a fast-changing, dynamic environment can only be met by good strategy. To survive in a dynamic, competitive market, you must play by the rules of competition. You must ignore internal desires.

If you let internal politics fester in your organization, everyone will become confused about your goals. Others will undermine confidence in your leadership. Politics will tear any organization apart and invite challenges from outside competitors. The more promising the potential of your organization, the more dangerous political conflicts become.

Establishing a clear mission is critical. It unites the different functions within an organization and focuses it on a shared goal. You must not weaken an enterprise's trust in its focus and purpose.

Minimizing the Initial Investment

A major theme continuing through the principles in this chapter is the idea of minimizing investments. A number of concepts cover ways to do this.

These methods flow directly from the problem of knowledge in competitive environments. What can you know for certain? You can know that don't have the resources to invest in every new opportunity. You can know that no one sells an insurance policy that guarantees success. While you cannot know how rewarding a new positions will be, you know for certain that your resources are limited. You know for certain that the efforts that you invest in a new, unproven positions must come from other parts of your life where you know the value.

These competitive principles teach us to think from the perspective on the long term. You cannot think that you can put more and more effort into a new position until it pays off. You must minimize your investments. Instead of investing, think about ways that you can make the position rewarding. Look for easy ways to make a position pay. Once you get more resources from a new position, you have invest more resources in developing that position. Even when you get rewarded, invest your limited resources only in what you absolutely need. This is the way you ensure that this new position will be rewarding.

Experimenting Locally

Many of Sun Tzu's minimization principles apply to distance. In our modern world, better communication and transportation have made the world smaller, but when you are exploring a new area, these principles teach us that is always best to start as close to home as you can. Moving away from your current position is just too expensive. If your experiments with new position are successful, they can always be broadened later.

This chapter's methdos look at the different ways in which distance can be costly. Travel and shipping are the costs of crossing geographic distance. Learning and communication are the costs of crossing intellectual distance. Learning about a new position distant from your own is expensive. Educating a new group of supporters who don't know you or your virtues is costly. High costs make it more difficult for a move to a position to reward us.

You want to test a new position as close to home as possible. Even new position can be close to home geographically or intellectually. Ideally, they are both. If the venture proves rewarding locally, you can then expand geographically as you increase your efficiency. If a new opportunity is too distant—either physically or intellectually—from what you are currently doing, you cannot afford to explore it.

Local Competitive Mismatch

Even though you start small, minimizing the size of your investment, you must be totally committed to the success of your position. Halfhearted efforts are certain to fail. When you work to minimize your mistakes, the only thing you cannot afford to minimize is the quality of your effort. You must persist in trying everything you can think of to make it work. You start small so you can overload the effort with resources.

The biggest danger in starting small is thinking that it doesn't matter if the venture succeeds or not. Just because you have put a minimum at risk never means you can afford to fail. It may take a hundred small failures to find a huge success, but you will never find that success if you don't put your best efforts into each attempt. In creating the light bulb, Edison failed again and again, but not because he was sloppy and disorganized.

Sure, many of these experiments with new positions will fail. You keep them small because of this real possibility of failure. Failure provides the best possible education if done correctly. A hundred productive failures teach you more precisely what works. A million sloppy, halfhearted failures get you no closer to your goal.

In the end, the principles in this volume teach that the overall size of your position or that of your competitors doesn't matter. It is the local mismatch, that is, the immediate comparison, that matters. If you are smaller than your competitors, you can more easily defend a smaller area. Positions with fewer resources are not powerful in comparison to the positions with a wealth of resources, but they can move much more quickly than their larger competitors. Large competitors cannot address the new situations as quickly as small ones can.

The principles in this chapter are important if you want to make all your new ventures pay for themselves as quickly as possible. You cannot plan how new positions will work out in the same way you can the operations of existing positions. These principles determines whether or not your new positions are successful or a threat to your future.

These rules teach us to focus on what you can do best. This means balancing your capabilities against those of your competitors. You may know your capabilities but not those of your competitors. Then for every successful new venture, another venture will fail. You can be ignorant of your abilities *and* those of your competitors. Then every new venture is doomed.

Mostly this volume of Sun Tzu's Playbook is about how you must minimize your mistakes. Success comes from knowing what needs to be done and what you can leave undone. Success comes from focusing your limited resources on new positions of the appropriate size.

5.0.0 Minimizing Mistakes

Sun Tzu's five keys for minimizing mistakes in advancing a position.

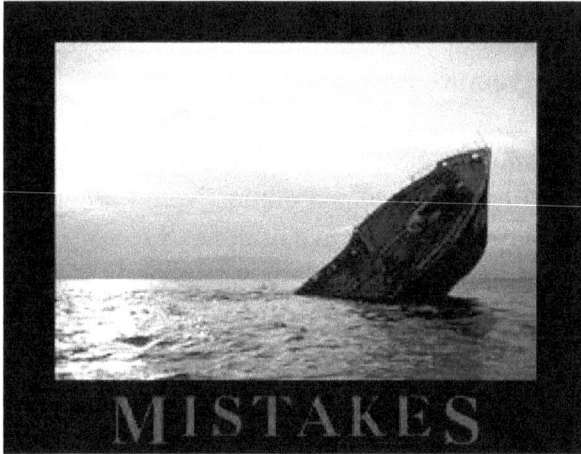

"Make good use of war.
Make the enemy's troops surrender.
You can do this fighting only minor battles."
                                Sun Tzu's The Art of War 3:3:1-3

"Never mistake motion for action."
                                Ernest Hemingway

General Principle: Our choice of action must minimize potential mistakes.

Situation:

This article begins a new section of The Playbook dealing with selecting the best way to pursue opportunities. Strategic moves are experiments. Our goal is to experiment safely. No matter how good our information and analysis, competitive environments are always uncertain and potentially treacherous. While we train to pick high-probability opportunities, we cannot delude ourselves about knowing those opportunities before exploring them directly. We must judge probabilities from surface appearances. We cannot understand the nature of an opportunity until we get into it. In using Sun Tzu's methods, nothing is as dangerous as investing too much in what seems like a certain opportunity.

Opportunity:

In choosing how to act to take advantage of opportunities, our first concern must be how we can minimize mistakes. Strategy requires both action and non-action. We must know when to act and when action is not only unnecessary but unwise. When we act, we must know how to increase the likely success of those actions while still minimizing the cost of our failures.

Key Methods:

The general key methods for making successful moves to advance our position are:

1. ***Successful actions serve our goals instead of simply responding to events and discoveries.*** This principle balances the prior one. While we must react to what we discover exploring opportunities rather that follow our plans, those reactions must be guided by our goals, taking us in a consistent direction. In exploring opportunities, we are going to make discoveries and encounter events that do not take us in the direction that we desire. Not all of these events and discoveries require or deserve a response. Not all discoveries demand exploration. Events that don't demand a reaction are merely distractions (5.1 Mission Priorities).

2. ***Successful actions explore opportunities instead of simply following plans.*** We must go where our opportunities lead us, not where we planned for them to lead us. It is easy for individuals and especially organizations to waste time and effort on executing campaign plans that are no longer relevant as more is learned about

a given opportunity. Plans can take on a life of their own if we let them. Plans start as a series of steps toward a goal, but the goal can move but the series of steps remains, offering us a seductive if unproductive path for our effort. Each move to take advantage of an opportunity must be thought of as an experiment. The key is to learn to experiment safely (5.2 Opportunity Exploration).

3. ***Successful actions are fast feedback loops adjusting our course of action.*** Successful actions are quickly chosen, quickly executed, and quickly adjusted. Competitive environments are highly dynamic. We must respond to situations quickly before those situations are outmoded by new developments. These quick adjustments also minimize opposition. Action usually generates resistance. The easiest way to minimize resistance from others is to change direction or reach our goals before opposition forms, ***fait accompli***. The faster we are able to move, the harder it is for opponents to get a fix on our position because the only information they have is outdated information (5.3 Reaction Time).

4. ***Successful actions eliminate waste.*** They use as few resources as possible to accomplish the desired goal. The best strategy is doing less, not more. Choose actions that simplify or minimize current activities rather than making them larger and more complicated (5.4 Minimizing Action).

5. ***Successful actions focus limited resources in a small space and time.*** Smaller, shorter, and quicker moves are always more successful more often than larger, longer, and slower moves. Small investments should prove themselves before investing more. The bigger the investment, the more difficult it is to admit failure. We attempt small, quick steps forward rather than large, long leaps. By choosing small, quick steps, we can sometimes end up making large leaps by getting ourselves positioned to use the force of the environment (5.5 Focused Power).

6. ***Successful actions know when to advance and when to defend.*** Even while we are exploring new opportunities, we must protect our current position. We advance our position on the basis of our strengths, but we must act to defend our position on the

basis of our weaknesses. The result is a balancing act balancing our resources between defense and advance (5.6 Defense and Advance).

Illustration:

The most frequent advance that more people make is getting a promotion at work so let us use that to illustrate these ideas.

1. ***Successful actions serve our goals instead of responding to events.*** Just because a new position opens up that is a promotion, we do not have to take it if it doesn't lead to the type of job we want.

2. ***Successful actions explore opportunities instead of simply following plans.*** We might have a certain career path in our heads, but that is not the path our career will follow. When we get out of school and join a company, we may imagine a certain promotion path, but most of our opportunities will not lie on that path.

3. ***Successful actions are fast feedback loops adjusting our course of action.*** Instead of thinking in formal job titles and pre-defined roles, think of a job in terms of responsibilities that can be added quickly to make others, including those over you, more dependent on your knowledge and skills.

4. ***Successful actions eliminate waste.*** One of the easiest ways to get recognition and promotion is by saving time, money, and effort by identifying resources that are currently being wasted by the organization.

5. ***Successful actions focus limited resources in a small space and time.*** The responsibilities don't have to be big ones, but little ones that accumulate over time. The best jobs are those that we define for ourselves over time by doing what is needed where our skills allow us to add the most value.

6. ***Successful actions know when to advance and when to defend.*** We must not let our expansions on our job get in the way of the core of what people expect from us. Over time, we must have

our new responsibilities formally recognized and get compensated for them.

5.1.0 Mission Priorities

Sun Tzu's five keys for aligning our actions with mission.

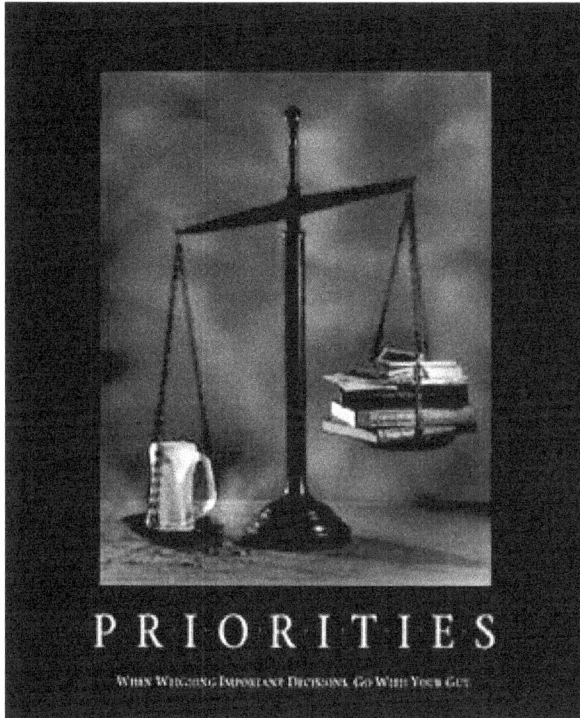

P R I O R I T I E S

WHEN WEIGHING IMPORTANT DECISIONS, GO WITH YOUR GUT

"Everything depends on your use of military philosophy."
Sun Tzu's The Art of War 2:1:1

"Before you begin climbing that ladder of success, make sure it's leaning towards the window of opportunity you desire!"

Tracy Brinkmann

General Principle: Actions that support our mission can be immediately gratifying but often aren't.

Situation:

Despite using our sophisticated mental models for picking high-probability opportunities, Sun Tzu's strategy cannot predict where an opportunity will lead. The strategic problem here is that, once we start pursuing an opportunity, that pursuit can take on a life of its own. Our choice of actions loses sight of our goals. We can choose actions because they are familiar, comfortable, and because we enjoy doing them. It would be wonderful if we could choose only actions that we enjoy on our path to success, but that is seldom the case.

Opportunity:

While we cannot always choose actions that are familiar, comfortable, and pleasurable, such actions do not necessarily conflict with our mission (1.6 Mission Values). As a matter of fact, we are more likely to make progress if our goals satisfy our short-term desires as well as our long-term values. However, we must also make that choice of action with a clear understanding of our range of our priorities (1.6.3 Mission Priorities). When we choose an action that satisfies many levels of motivation, both our own and our supporters, our chances of success increase greatly.

Key Methods:

The key methods concerning the use of mission to guide our choice of actions offer both serious warning and intriguing possibilities.

1. We must choose actions that conform with our values. This means not only that our actions must move us toward our mission, but it also means that our actions must always be consistent with our values. 2,500 year ago, Sun Tzu taught that the most important thing about our methods is that they must conform with our values. The best time to ask question about the ultimate value of actions is before we begin. Once we have chosen a course of action, it is always more difficult, costly, and sometimes even dangerous to abandon it ([1.6 Mission Values]).

2. We want to choose actions that address immediate desires and move us toward longer-term goals. Short-term gratification (happiness) and long-term goals (meaning) are not incompatible. Research shows that those who have more of one also find more of the other. Ideally, we want to choose actions that satisfy both at once. There are many levels to the motivations that drive us. Sun Tzu's strategy is, by its nature, a long-term view, but it recognizes our short-term needs. Our longterm success from purposeful action is more certain if we can stay on the right path, but we cannot stay on that path if we make the journey too difficult. We need pleasurable activities as well. We must avoid short-term activities that block our longer-term prospects and we must also avoid choosing long-term courses that are so disagreeable that we cannot sustain our progress ([1.6.2 Types of Motivations]).

3. We must choose actions that are disagreeable that satisfy our long-term mission. As we move toward our goals, at some point, we are going to get into areas that are unfamiliar, uncomfortable, and unpleasant. This is the price we pay for wanting to advance ourselves. Actively making progress simply is never as easy as drifting where life takes us. Since we have limited resources, we must choose how to invest them. We can either put them into immediately gratification or we can invest them in our longer term goals. Making sacrifices today is a gift that we give our future selves. As actions that were once difficult become familiar, more comfortable, they naturally become more pleasant, decreasing their costs in effort over time ([3.1.2 Strategic Profitability]).

4. Events are no excuse for forgetting our mission or violating our values. We cannot use events as an excuse. Events are going to continue to happen. We must continually choose which require response, which are external distractions, and which are deadly short-cuts. Our actions have costs but they also have consequences. "Short-cuts" that can seemingly take us toward our goal by cheating on our values run the risk of cutting us off from success completely. Actions that are often the most tempting in terms of potential return are often the most costly in terms of values (5.1.1 Event Pressure).

5. *Existing habits, practices, and procedures must be continually re-evaluated in terms of mission.* Many of our activities are part of our internal system of production. While all our activities originally create some external benefit, these activities can continue past their usefulness. They continue out of internal inertia while external needs change. After a point, they can consume our tlimited resources while producing no benefit satisfying our short-term or long-term goals. To prevent this from happening, we must regularly reevaluate repeated activities to maintain their connection with mission (5.1.2 Internal Distraction).

Illustration:

Let us consider the simplest of all goals, making money. t

1. *We must choose actions that conform with our values*. Even if our goal is making money, we cannot simply lie to get it, steal it from people, or become a politician, but I am being redundant.

2. *We want to choose actions that address immediate desires and move us toward longer-term goals.* If we can make money doing something that we like because people find it valuable, for example, writing and teaching Sun Tzu's strategy, we should do it. We cannot make money enjoying ourselves, say, by writing songs, because too many others are willing to write songs for free.

3. *Often, we must choose actions that are disagreeable that satisfy our long-term mission.* To get to a point where we can make money doing what we like, we have to do certain things that are unpleasant, such as going out and selling ourselves and promoting our work.

4. *Events are no excuse for forgetting our mission or violating our values.* If we get an email offering us millions simply for helping a professional gentleman get some money out of Nigeria a little bit illegally, we shouldn't go for it, no matter how wealthy it will make us.

5. Existing habits, practices, and procedures must be continually re-evaluated in terms of mission. For example, I am working on these articles daily, do they get me closer to my goals? Fortunately, my goal is not simply making money but building a lasting body of work.

5.1.1 Event Pressure

Sun Tzu's eight keys for avoiding mistakes under the pressure of events.

> *"Internal and external events force people to move. They are unable to work while on the road."*
>
> Sun Tzu's The Art of War 13:1:6

> *"When I can't handle events, I let them handle themselves."*
>
> Henry Ford

General Principle: Mission guides us about how to respond to the pressure of events.

Situation:

This article will never be finished because events keep intruding. Just joking. One of the biggest challenges in undertaking actions to pursue opportunities is the pressure of events. Unless we remain focused on our mission, events can rob us of our ability to choose our actions. Events create the "ringing telephone" problem. We cannot know if the call is valuable or not without answering it, but the probability of value is remote while the cost of disruption is certain. We often seem helpless to choose our actions in the face of events. Events come to us, knock on our door and keep demanding our attention. They can even seem to demand specific actions that leave us little choice but to respond. If our lives become a series of ringing phones, we have no time left over to do anything but answer and answer endlessly.

Opportunity:

Good choices about responding or not responding to events can become an automatic reflex. As our training in Sun Tzu's strategy progresses, our focus becomes more fixed on our mission and we develop the appropriate filters to automatically eliminate distractions while noticing what must be noticed. Inaction is a legitimate choice to of response to events. We can train ourselves to recognize which events demand a response and which do not. This is important because, under the pressure of events, we don't have time to consciously decide (6.1.1 Conditioned Reflexes). Just as we can train ourselves to see opportunities that are usually hidden, we can also train ourselves to automatically reject events that do not require a response.

Key Methods:

The following are the key methods for dealing with event pressure, filtering out distractions while responding to events that demand a response.

1. We must always listen to events. Strategy means respond-ing to the outside environment. We cannot cut ourselves off from events, at least not for any meaningful period of time. In the Prog-ress Cycle of listen-aim-move-claim, the listening is constant. We must always be listening so we can always be adjusting to events. We cannot know when the event demanding our attention is a criti-cal one or not unless we at least listen. The choice is when we move, that is, respond to events. (1.8 Progress Cycle).

2. Because we always listen we must constantly choose action or non-action. In the world of production , we are trained to follow orders so listening implies responding. In the competitive world, our success depends on our making our own decisions about when to act. Since we are always listening, we must constantly choose whether or not to respond. In the terminology of strategy, we are always aiming as well. This means that we have to retrain ourselves to recognize non-action as the most common appropriate response (4.2 Choosing Non-Action).

3. The more events we respond to, the more events we will trigger. In some situations, we may want to create more events and interaction with our environment. In other situations, creating more events simply create more distractions. We must filter out fewer events if we want more interaction and filter out more events if we want less interaction. We must constantly be aware if these events and responses are taking us closer to our goals or further away (2.3.1 Action and Reaction).

4. We must filter out events that don't affect us. Inside a pro-ductive organization, most messages we receive are aimed at us personally and therefore require a response. Outside, in the larger competitive world, most events have nothing to do with us, our strategic position, and our competitive neighborhood can be safely ignored. While these events may be interesting, satisfying our curiosity is a very short-term desire that needs to conform with our longer term goals (5.1 Mission Priorities).

5. We must filter out events that our actions cannot affect. Even if an event affects us or our position, there are many events where our actions cannot change anything. We cannot use the event to advance our position or defend our position. Events that we cannot use or affect can be ignored (5.6 Defense and Advance).

6. We must notice which events that demand action now. Even if an event affects us and can be used by our actions, those actions usually don't have to be performed immediately. What we cannot ignore are events that demand immediate action. These events fall into two categories 1) attacks or challenges that will get worse with delay and 2) opportunities which will soon disappear (5.6.2 Acting Now).

7. We must filter out events if we lack the resources to respond. Even if events require action now, we don't necessarily have the resources necessary to respond. Often the issue here is the size of the response required. Events that demand a small response are much easier to deal with because the resources are more readily available. The gap between other tasks on our stack gives us little pieces of time to respond to events without distraction. (3.1.1 Resource Limitations).

8. We must balance what we are doing now against the value of responding to the event. This brings us back to the core idea of our mission determining our priorities. Even if an event requires immediate action, responding to it isn't necessarily as important as completing our current task. Even timely events, if they can prevent us from accomplishing anything if we let them. We must balance acting now in response to an event against completing the task (move) at hand. The only way to compare the two actions and decide which best serves our goals (1.6 Mission Values).

Illustration:

Today, we live in a world of communication devices, many of which can create very bad habits in terms of event pressure. Cell phones, texting, email, instant messaging, Internet searches and Twitter all present different challenges. Let us briefly illustrate these principles in the context of modern communication to highlight some of the issue.

1. We must always listen to events. All these tool expand our ability to listen. ringing cell phone demands attention, but caller ID and messaging systems alleviate the pressure of responding now. However, tools such as instant messaging create problems because, by logging in, we are saying we are available.

2. Because we always listen we must constantly choose action or non-action. We do not have to respond to every email or text message. As a matter of fact, doing so can become a time-wasting addiction.

3. The more events we respond to, the more events we will trigger. Respond to every text message increases the number of texts that we get. The same if true of every other form of communication.

4. We must filter out events that don't affect us. A given Twitter stream may be interesting and entertaining, but most are strategically useless.

5. We must filter out events that our actions cannot affect. We may be upset or excited about what celebrities or politicians (am I repeating myself?) are doing, but these "events" are well beyond our arena of action.

6. We must notice events that demand action now. If we get a call from our mother, we better answer because nothing is as important as a mother's love.

7. We must filter out events if we lack the resources to respond. I would really like to help out that guy in Nigeria with all that money stuck in a bank, but my time is limited.

8. We must balance what we are doing now against the value of responding to the event. I found that, as my software company grew to over a hundred employees, I no longer owned the company. It owned me. My time was no longer my own. The issue was which customer, employee, or partner had the most pressing claim on my time. I ended up doing what I felt was important in the evening or when I was traveling.

5.1.2 Unproductive Responsibility

Sun Tzu's seven keys for understanding how our planned activities develop a life of their own.

*"Supporting the military makes the nation powerful.
Not supporting the military makes the nation weak."*
Sun Tzu's The Art of War 3:4:3-4

*"Never again clutter your days or nights with so many
menial and unimportant things that you have no time
to accept a real challenge when it comes along. This
applies to play as well as work. A day merely survived
is no cause for celebration. You are not here to fritter
away your precious hours when you have the ability
to accomplish so much by making a slight change in
your routine. No more busy work. No more hiding from
success. Leave time, leave space, to grow. Now. Now!
Not tomorrow!"*

Og Mandino

General Principle: Productive responsibilities must be measured against competitive mission.

Situation:

Our existing responsibilities can act as a serious barrier to progress. Unfortunately, in the world of production, we tend to see our responsibilities in terms of a list of specific activities rather than a set of general goals. That list of opportunities can grow until it leaves room for little else. These activities may have value in the larger scheme of things, but they may not. We commit to doing many tasks that have minimal value and tasks that were valuable can cease to have value. Sun Tzu's principles in this area are designed to keep unproductive commitments to a minimum.

Opportunity:

If we keep focused on our mission, finding time to pursue new opportunities should become a regular part of our workload rather than an intrusion upon it. We pursue new opportunities when we have the "excess" resources, but we must continually cultivate those resources (3.3 Opportunity Resources). If we regularly evaluate our activities against our mission, we will have the time and resources when an opportunity comes along (5.1 Mission Priorities).

Key Methods:

The following are the key methods for dealing with the pressure of our daily responsibilities, filtering out low value activities that do not service our mission.

1. An activity can fall within our span of control without being productive. The difference between competition and production is explained in this series of public articles. Competition wins control of ground. Production harvest resources from that ground. However, just because an activity falls within the realm of productive planning , it doesn't automatically mean that that activity itself is productive. Within our span of control, internal routines and procedures are developed that serve the needs of current competition, but as those external needs change, those responsibilities can continue without producing value (1.9 Competition and Production).

2. Planned productive activities must produce resources to defend _and_ advance our position. We not only want to hold our current position but we want to improve it over time. Value is defined by our mission, that is, our goals and values. We plan activities within our span of control to produce value. The ultimate end of strategy is to secure more potential productive capacity. The ultimate end of production is to produce more resources for competition (8.1.1 Transforming Resources).

3. Planned activities and responsibilities can easily lose sight _of competitive mission_. We can live our lives devoting more and more of our time to our controlled activities. We feel more secure within this bubble of control. From working within this bubble, we develop methods that work to best discharge our responsibilities. This gives us the illusion of control. We start to think that only what happens inside of our span of control is important. We lose sight of the fact that our mission goals always lie outside our control (1.7.2 Goal Focus).

4. Our productive responsibilities can not lose contact with _events_. Our position is never secure. Events outside of our control constantly affect our position. All existing positions are temporary. We cannot cut ourselves off from responding to events, that is, making strategic moves, at least nto for any meaningful period of time. We must not only pay attention to external events but be prepared to respond to them when necessary (1.1.1 Position Dynamics).

5. We must prioritize planned internal activities by their _production of external value_. We must use the yardstick of our competitive goals. From those values, we must understand which activities are high-value and which have low value. If we are assigned low-value duties, we must work to get those responsibilities dropped or transferred elsewhere. If we perform even the most routine tasks with a sense of the value they produce, the better we are able to balance our use of time (5.1 Mission Priorities).

6. We must do the most valuable productive tasks first. The production of value follows the law of diminishing returns. We cannot afford to perform every productive activity, no matter how slight its value. Our first priority is defending our current position because our current position provides the starting point for our future progress. So we must do those tasks that maintaining our positions absolutely requires. However, our productive work must also create the excess resources to pursue future opportunities. This means that we cannot use all our time and efforts on value production alone (5.6.1 Defense Priority , 3.3 Opportunity Resources).

7. Split our limited resources between production and competition based on our opportunities. Our resources are always limited. During periods of limited opportunities, we must focus more of those resources on maintaining our current position. During period of high-opportunity, we must shift our use of resources to advancing our position. However, we must always split our resources between both arenas. Using the 80/20 Pareto Principle and shifting the 80% in the required direction in a given position is a useful rule of thumb. This means that we should never use less that 20% of our resources on improving our position, serving our long term mission (3.1.1 Resource Limitations).

Illustration:

Let us illustrate these principles by applying them to a internal productive role, accounting, and an external competitive role, selling. The contrast between the two very different types of roles is instructive.

1. An activity can fall within our span of control without being productive. Both salespeople and accountant can be required to do certain activities, such as producing specific reports, that once served an important competitive purpose but, over time, have lost their value.

2. Planned productive activities must produce resources to defend __and__ advance our position. An accountant primarily works to defend a position by providing information on current financial status and trends, but they must also help advance position by cost controls that save money that make the organization more cost competitive. A salesperson works primarily to advance a competitive position by winning new customers but must also defend position by maintaining existing customers.

3. Planned activities and responsibilities can easily lose sight of competitive mission. An accounting procedure or report can be established to address a given accounting or tax rule but continue after that rule changes. A salesperson can continue to service an existing customer long after that customer has ceased to be profitable.

4. Our productive responsibilities can not lose contact with events. Accountants must know when tax, accounting, and management demands that require account work change. Salespeople must know when a customer or product status changes.

5. We must prioritize planned internal activities by their production of external value. Accountants should know which of their reports are the most valuable for management decisions. Salespeople should know which customers and products are the most profitable.

6. We must do the most valuable productive tasks first. Accountants must first work on getting the most valuable information out quickly and correctly. Salespeople must first focus on selling their more profitable products to their most profitable customers.

7. Split our limited resources between production and competition based on our opportunities. All accountants must spend some of their time evaluating the value of the reports they produce. All salespeople must spend some of their time maintaining existing customers before going after new ones.

5.2 Opportunity Exploration

Sun Tzu's seven keys regarding a mental framework for exploring opportunities.

"Make no assumptions about all the dangers in using military force.
Then you won't make assumptions about the benefits of using arms either."

Sun Tzu's The Art of War 2:2:1-2

"There's an element of exploration. You are always looking over the hill [to] what's next."

James Reilly

General Principle: Exploration of opportunities requires more commitment than planning.

Situation:

Choosing the best way to explore an opportunity is less a matter of planning than experimenting. We can think about various courses our exploration might take, but the actual course that it does take depends on what we find along the way. If we commit ourselves to a specific series of preplanned steps rather than exploration itself, we are making a mistake before we begin. Planning assumes control. Competitive environments are beyond our control because they are complex, dynamic, and chaotic. The thought that we can pre-plan our explorations of competitive environment misses the whole point of exploration.

Opportunity:

When we commit ourselves to exploration, we commit to the unknown. When we explore opportunities, we work in undiscovered territory (3.2 Opportunity Creation). Opportunities are "openings" because no one knows what they contain. By definition, we cannot predict what conditions we will find. We explore opportunities to discover those conditions. Exploration of opportunities takes us beyond the limits of traditional planning.

Key Methods:

The following key methods provide the best mental frame for thinking about activities to explore and opportunity.

1. When an opportunity is explored, no one knows what we will find. Our plans are based upon what we think can happen. Since so much can happen in an unknown environment, our plans naturally expand. We try to consider all possibilities, and that leads to making more alternative plans. The longer we try to perfect our plans, the more costly our new venture becomes in terms of the time and effort we have put into it without learning anything. While we are busy planning, we are not exploring the situation and learning about it (3.1.5 Unpredictable Value).

2. When an opportunity is explored, our activities test the ground. When we explore opportunities, we are just testing them. We take a few steps in a given direction to see if it is viable. Instead of thinking about developing opportunities through a series of activities, the first step is thinking of a way to test their value. The best activity demonstrates simply whether or not an opportunity is worth developing further. The activities we choose should quickly prove only that an opportunity is worthy of further resources (5.4.1 Value Tests).

3. To explore opportunities, we start with the simplest possible experiment. It is never wise to start with a big, complex experiment. Big complex experiments require a lot of resources and have a lot of moving parts. They involve too many variables and require a lot of planning and control. Planning and control are rare in competitive environments. Instead, we start with the simplest possible steps in the direction of the opportunity to see what arises. If those first few steps prove fruitful, we can then scale up our activities (5.0 Minimizing Mistakes).

4. Exploring opportunities requires general deadlines and goals rather than specific ones. In controlled, production environments, we have very specific goals in the form of some-type of product specification. From that specification, we can determine exact resources needed. Since we specify the exact product, we can design, organize our production process, and set firm deadlines for production. Our goals in exploring an opportunity must be more general because an opportunity is never specific. We know only that is is an opening, a hole that we might be able to fill. We must discover its shape by exploration in order to see how we can fill it. From that exploration, we start to put together product specifications not before (3.1.4 Openings).

5. When we are exploring an opportunity, we must make many of our decisions in the moment. Our decisions depend on what we find. Our moves test openings. From a distance, we only know the surface of these openings but we don't know their true shape. We must follow the shape of the opening to understand it. Sun Tzu called this letting the ground dictate our methods (3.2.1 Environmental Dominance).

6. The more we plan opportunity exploration, the more unwarranted assumptions we make. When we think in terms of major expeditions with specific goals, we want to develop more detailed plans. We think that the more detailed our plan, the safer our new venture is. The opposite is true. All of the assumptions that we must make to create those plans are meaningless because they have not been tested. The longer we plan, the more we think of our assumptions as true and the more we expose ourselves to uncertainty (2.1.2 Leveraging Uncertainty),

7. The more we execute a plan instead of freely exploring opportunities, the further we fall behind our competition. While we are planning grand expeditions, our competitors can take simple steps exploring the territory to see what works. It doesn't matter how smart we think we are. We can't get ahead by falling behind. The secret is finding out a little more about the opportunity and quickly adapt our future activities to what we have learned (1.8.3 Cycle Time).

Illustration:

Let us illustrate these principles by applying them to exploring the opportunity for training people in strategy using games instead of traditional classroom education techniques.

1. When an opportunity is explored, no one knows what we will find. People may like the idea of a game. People may not. Useful games may be easy to develop or very difficult. Board games may be better than card games. We simply do not know what the opportunity holds.

2. When an opportunity is explored, our activities test the ground. We want to test this idea by getting some games out for people to try.

3. To explore opportunities, we start with the simplest possible experiment. Instead of developing games from scratch, we want to adapt existing games to teach strategic principles. Since many games teach strategy, we can adapt a few to make those lessons clearer and teach standard terminology.

4. Exploring opportunities requires general deadlines and goals rather than specific ones. We will start looking at various games an how they might simply be adapted. We want to get initial versions into people's hands as quickly as possible but not as finished products as much as tests of the concepts.

5. When we are exploring an opportunity, we must make many of our decisions in the moment. We may be looking at a game that we heard about as useful, but in search for that game, we must find a completely different game that is even better suited to our purposes. The StratUnity Card Game came about in just this way. We were looking at one card game, reading reviews and someone mention an older, similar game that became the basis of Stratunity.

6. The more we plan opportunity exploration, the more unwarranted assumptions we make. While our goals may be to automate our training games, putting them on hand-devices and allowing members to have tournaments on-line, we want to make sure that those games work before making the investment.

7. The more we execute a plan instead of freely exploring opportunities, the further we fall behind our competition. Our primary focus is on first creating a complete set of principles worthy of learning. The more effort we put at this point in developing more sophisticated game platforms, the more that work will be delayed.

5.2.1 Choosing Adaptability

Sun Tzu's five key methods for choosing actions that allow us a maximum of future flexibility.

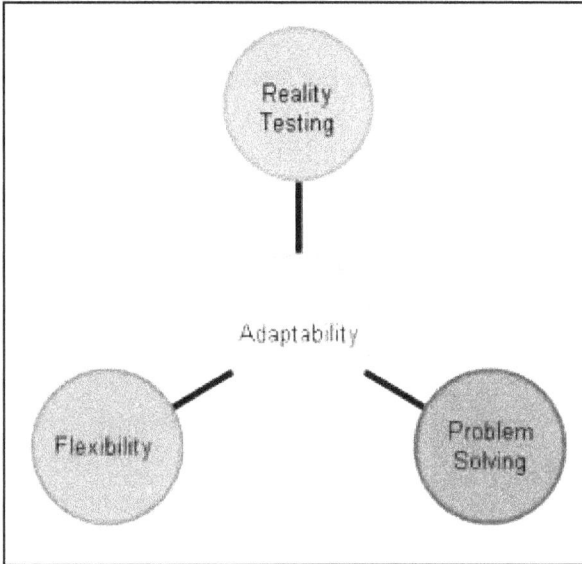

"Make war without a standard approach.
Water has no consistent shape."
Sun Tzu's The Art of War, 6:8:8-9

"All fixed set patterns are incapable of adaptability or pliability. The truth is outside of all fixed patterns."
Bruce Lee

General Principle: We must choose actions that allow us to best respond to unknown conditions and unforeseen events.

Situation:

Adaptability requires the ability to move in a new direction at any time. Exploring an opportunity means expecting unforeseen discoveries (3.1.5 Unpredictable Value). Exploration takes time so we must be prepared for unforeseen events to occur (2.3.2 Reaction Unpredictability). We must choose our initial actions so that we can easily adapt them to emerging circumstances. Success in moving to new positions requires both our commitment to the goal and flexibility as to our methods. Our goal of exploring an opportunity remains the same, but we want to be free to choose a different path of exploration at any time.

Opportunity:

When we commit ourselves to exploration, we commit to the unknown. When we explore opportunities, we work in undiscovered territory (3.2 Opportunity Creation). Opportunities are "openings" because no one knows what they contain. By definition, we cannot predict what conditions we will find. We explore opportunities to discover those conditions. Exploration of opportunities takes us beyond the limits of traditional planning.

Key Methods:

In choosing how to explore an activity, we must keep the following key methods in mind.

1. To use adaptability, we must expect anything and everything. We have to admit to ourselves that we do not know what we will find when we explore an opportunity. Exploring an opening requires opening ourselves up to the possibilities. Discovery always lies outside of our expectations and assumptions. This is the fun and excitement and terror of real strategy. Any given step may lead onward or to a dead-end. It may lead to fortune of failure. We commit ourselves to taking the next step with this in mind (5.2 Opportunity Exploration).

2. To improve our adaptability, we choose initial activities that give us a better vantage point. From a better vantage point, we can get the lay of the land. Every step forward into an opening is experimental. The goal of the experiment is to discover more about the opportunity. With a broader point of view, we can pick better and better follow-up activities to explore the terrain we discover (2.4.1 Ground Perspective).

3. To maintain our adaptability, we choose activities that allow adjustment to unexpected events. We must prepare ourselves not only for discovering more but for what we already know to change. We must choose initial actions that gives us the greatest possible flexibility to adapt to these unforeseen events. Situations will change in expected ways. Especially when opportunities require us to navigate difficult ground forms, we must choose activities that minimize the common types of problems we will encounter from climate shifts ((1.4.1 Climate Shift , 4.3 Ground Forms).

4. To improve our adaptability, we choose directions that open up new options. Exploration is a learning activity. Every choice closes some doors, but when we have the option, we should pick activities that open more doors than they close. To do this, the best activities usually get us over a small barrier that obstructs other options (4.5.2 Opportunity Barriers).

5. To get the most out of our adaptability, we must leverage the conditions we find. A journey of a thousand miles always starts with a single step, but there is an inherent difference between traveling a well-mapped route and exploring unknown territory. Adapting to an opportunity means taking what the situation gives us. In a sense, our initial steps are experiments to discover the path of least resistance. We only have limited resources and we don't want to waste them tackling challenges until we have looked for a way around them (1.8.2 The Adaptive Loop).

Illustration:

Let us illustrate these ideas with the simple analogy of choosing to right vehicle to explore unknown terrain.

1. To use adaptability, we must expect anything and every-thing. We don't buy a train ticket to explore unknown terrain. We don't want an ordinary car, even if the road looks smooth. We want a rugged four-wheel drive SUV with good visibility all around because we don't know what we will find.

2. To improve our adaptability, we choose initial activities that give us a better vantage point. Since there are no roads, we want to choose a route that works its way up a hill to get the lay of the land.

3. To maintain our adaptability, we choose activities that allow adjustment to unexpected events. We don't go into narrow ravines where a rock fall might block us or a rain storm could flood us. We don't cross rivers where we might get stuck or hit unexpected currents.

4. To improve our adaptability, we choose directions that open up new options. We head for areas where the underbrush looks thinner, rocks fewer, the ground more even, less sticky, and slippery.

5. To get the most out of our adaptability, we must leverage the conditions we find. While we can get over the rocks or fallen trees blocking our path, we first try to find a way around them.

5.2.2 Campaign Methods

Sun Tzu's five key methods describing the use of campaigns and their methods.

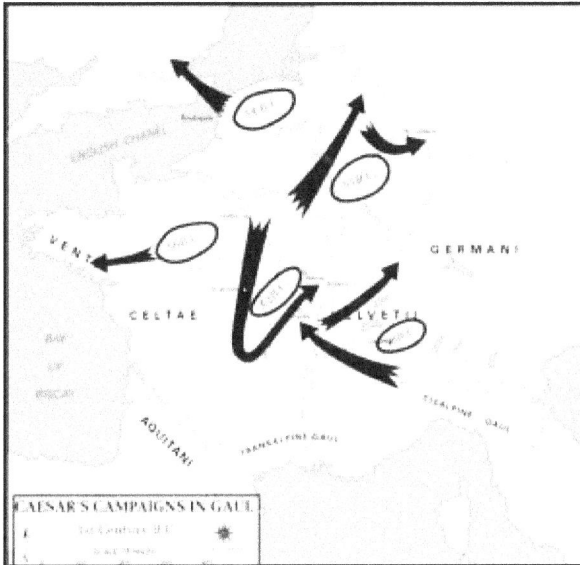

CAESAR'S CAMPAIGNS IN GAUL

> *"Fight five different campaigns without a firm rule for victory."*
>
> Sun Tzu's The Art of War 6:8:12

> *"Life is a campaign not a battle, and has its defeats as well as its victories."*
>
> Don Piatt

General Principle: Campaigns use a variety of methods to combine smaller moves toward a longer-term goal.

Situation:

A campaign is a series or group of related actions or moves used to take advantage of an opportunity. In a campaign, we use a series of short-term positions to attain a longer term position that we desire.

Campaigns are necessary because many opportunities cannot be pursued by a single move but rather in a series of stages. The fact that related moves can be tied together, leads, unfortunately, to much of the confusion between planning and strategy. Changing circumstances can easily make both plans and campaigns irrelevant, but that fact cannot let us ignore this powerful tool of strategy.

Opportunity:

As long as we continually re-evaluate the value of a given campaign, campaigns can serve as a powerful tool (6.2 Campaign Evaluation). The use of campaigns allow us to break down our progress toward a goal into a series of smaller, more certain steps (5.5 Focused Power). A good understanding of campaigns can help us identify how to best take advantage of an opportunity and our alternatives when a given move fails.

Key Methods:

The following key methods describe the methods campaigns use to take advantage of an opportunity.

1. A campaign is a series of related actions used to take advantage of an opportunity. The open positions targeted by campaigns cannot be achieved by a single move. They are usually positions that are well-defined, well-established, and persistent. They therefore require a series of related, small actions. The relationships among these moves can take a variety of forms. Though we can think about the potential shape a given campaign *may* take, in the end the actual shape of the campaign will be determined not by our plans, but by the result of each move (5.2.1 Choosing Adaptability).

2. Campaigns are required to cover large distances and/or get around significant barriers. In our daily decision-making, we often filter out opportunities that require large investment in time and effort because those opportunities are less likely to lead to success. Since some well-defined and established positions are more persistent than regular opportunities, the nature of a competitive landscape can simply require a group of related moves to establish these positions (4.5 Opportunity Surfaces).

3. A campaign can divide a large, risky move into a safer series of incremental actions. Using this method, each move depends on the others. Each move gets us a little closer to our goal, building on the progress of all the previous actions in the series. Each move addresses a separate aspect or issue of the opportunity. These issues are defined by the nature of the opportunity, what must be learned and controlled. The exact nature of each action cannot be known precisely beforehand since it depends on the result of the previous action. The series of actions method gets its strength from our ability to focus on single smaller actions at a time (5.4 Minimizing Action).

4. A campaign can break down a large barrier with the cumulative, convergent effect of small actions. Some campaigns rely upon mounting effects separate, independent actions. Each action, by itself, is not sufficient to achieve the desired goal. Indeed, each action may be in many ways considered a "failure" because it appears not to make any difference in our situation. However, the impact of these actions mount over time. While each action doesn't get us measurably closer to our goal in incremental sense, it does build up the pressure that eventually wins the desired position (6.8.2 Strength in Adversity).

5. A campaign can persistently pursue a sequence of alternative paths one after another. Using this method, each move independently explores a different path until we find one that works. Each of these paths, if successful, could get us to our goal by itself. These paths are parallel, not a series of steps or a cumulative effort. We do not to pursue these alternative paths at the same time. Each failure may or may not teach us about where to look for the next.

We try one after a other until we find the one the works (1.9 Competition and Production).

Illustration:

Since we are talking about a variety of different uses of campaigns, let us describe a variety of different types of campaign.

1. A campaign is a series of related actions used to take advantage of an opportunity. We all start our lives with the campaign called "getting an eduction." For some of us, that campaign never stops.

2. Campaigns are required to cover large distances and/or get around significant barriers. Campaigns are required to get a college degree, get licensed in a profession, win elected office, or build a successful company.

3. A campaigns can divide a large, risky move into a safer series of incremental actions. We are developing this Strategic Playbook using this campaign method. First, we created the outline of strategic topics. Then we created the initial articles to fill in that outline. Now we update those articles to detail the principles involved and meet a certain standard. Finally, we can develop training and certification procedures around the resulting body of knowledge. Completing each step was and is necessary before we can proceed to the next.

4. A campaign can break down a large barrier with the cumulative, convergent effect of small actions. The best example of this technique was the political career of Abraham Lincoln. Lincoln ran for a series of offices, losing every election. However, the cumulative affect of his campaigns was to eventually win the presidency.

5. A campaigns can persistently pursue a sequence of alternative paths one after another. This method largely describes Edison's search for the right filament to create the electric light. He simply tried different materials in sequence until he found one that worked.

5.2.3 Unplanned Steps

Sun Tzu's seven key methods distinguishing campaign adjustments from steps in a plan.

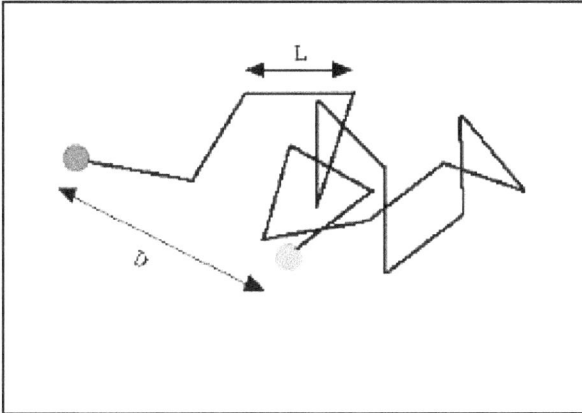

"You must be creative in your strategy.
You must adapt to your opportunities and weaknesses."
Sun Tzu's The Art of War 8:2:1-2

"No battle plan survives contact with the enemy."
Colin Powell

"When we are sure that we are on the right road there is no need to plan our journey too far ahead. No need to burden ourselves with doubts and fears as to the obstacles that may bar our progress. We cannot take more than one step at a time."
Orison Swett Marden

"A good plan violently executed now is better than a perfect plan next week."
General George S. Patton

General Principle: A campaign is a series of separate adjustments not a pre-planned series of commitments.

Situation:

Our plans have gravity. That gravity can capture us. It can trap us without our even being aware of it. Like a planet speeding around a star, we think we are going somewhere when we are really going in circles. The gravity of plans, like the gravity of the stars and planets, is determined by their size. The larger and more massive a plan is, the more it tends to control our direction and shape our view of reality. People mistakenly think that the more detailed their planning is, the more likely it is that their plans will be successful. While this is true in production environments, the opposite is always true in competitive environments.

Opportunity:

While strategic campaigns can require many separate steps, we cannot confuse a campaign with a plan. Our opportunity is to get away from the word "planning" entirely when considering competitive advances. Like the word, "strategy," people use the word "planning," to describe many different types of activities. George Patton, growing up in a less linear era , used the term to mean setting general objectives in a campaign. A campaign sets aside resources to surmount a specific obstacle (6.2 Campaigns). Colin Powell, a product of a more linear education system , sees planning as a series of steps to produce a well-defined result. It is this later approach to planning that works against good strategy as General Powell realized.

Key Methods:

The key methods for making sure we are choosing the best activities based on adaptive strategy rather than planned commitments are as follows:

1. In outlining a campaign, we must see each component as a separate test. Since competitive campaigns can overlap with productive plans, we must distinguish between regions of internal control and regions of external competition. Separating linear planning from adaptive strategy is difficult because we are constantly shifting between the two realms. Working within our areas of control, we often formulate plans beyond the event horizon of our control. We must always question ourselves about just where we are crossing the line (1.9 Competition and Production).

2. Planned steps are comforting tasks while a strategic action is an invigorating challenge. By "invigorating," we mean a little nerve-racking. Strategic action always has an air of uncertainty because it is a probabilistic not deterministic process. If an action seems comfortable and certain, it is a plan, not strategic action. We cannot let the comforting nature of plans draw us into making the wrong competitive decisions in the realm of uncontrolled events. If the way we think about the step leaves open the possibility of failure, it is a strategic activity (1.8.4 Probabilistic Process).

3. *We should not feel pressure to act only to satisfy our own expectations.* This means we shouldn't feel any need to do what we thought we might do. The more we use linear plans, the more invested we become to our plans. The more pressure we feel to perform a certain action simply because we expected to perform it. We must escape from the gravity of planning. Any pressure we feel should come from the external situation, not from our planning (3.2.1 Environmental Dominance).

4. We should feel the pressure of cycle time and events not deadlines. Time pressure should come from the window of opportunity closing and our desire to learn. When we plan, we naturally think about deadlines for synchronizing tasks. In an competitive environment, completing many tasks is beyond our control, as we will soon discover. As we start to execute our plan, we cross into the region outside of our control (3.1.6 Time Limitations).

5. Progress means getting environment feedback not checking off to-do items. Working through a plan, we feel like we are making progress when we finish our to-do list. Strategic actions only recognizes progress in the form of learning about the environment, ideally about how we can make exploration pay. If we commit to a direction without getting rewarding feedback from the environment, we can keep heading in a wrong and potentially fatal direction (1.8.3 Cycle Time).

6. Each step is based upon the results of the last step. We constantly update our picture of the situation, adjusting our priorities and time-line to what we learn. The results of all these areas of testing are factored in to the moves that we make. In terms of the listen-aim-move-claim progress cycle, we should listen in all these areas at once before aiming and moving in any of them. Maintaining this flexible and adaptive mindset is the key to our competitive success (1.8 Progress Cycle).

7. Each step may be revisited based upon the results of the next step. This is not a linear process. The discoveries in a later step may require us to revisit an earlier activity. The process is a loop and the nature of the loop is based upon all the outcomes involved (1.8.2 The Adaptive Loop).

Illustration:

This article was written largely because most "business plans," such as those taught in business school and encouraged by banks, make mockery of good strategy. To illustrate this principle, imagine that we see an opportunity for opening a new restaurant in a fast-growing neighborhood. What does the campaign to open that restaurant look like?

1. In outlining a campaign, we must see each component as a separate test. If we thought that controlled the business environment, we might make a plan that looks like this:

- find a good location,
- decorate the restaurant,
- develop a menu,
- get equipment and supplies, and hire and train a staff.

Looks reasonable, but since we don't control the market for a restaurant, a strategic campaign outline for opening a restaurant looks similar to a linear plan, but it is really a series of adaptive and dependent loops:

- We test the market for a good location;
- We test interior designs against strengths of the location;
- We test the menu against the location;
- We test the marketplace for equipment and ingredients; and
- We test the market for a staff and what training is required.

2. *Planned steps are comforting while strategic action should be invigorating*. See how reassuring the first list looks? The process seems simply, like building a machine. The second list makes it clear everything is uncertain. There may not be any good location. Many designs may not work in the location we find. The menu depends on the location we find and what the competition in the area already offers. The second list is a list of challenges not tasks.

3. *We should not feel pressure to act only to satisfy our own expectations*. We might have envisioned opening a fancy Italian restaurant, but the situation may well call for a small neighborhood bistro.

4. *We should feel the pressure of cycle time and events not deadlines*. We need to find a location, but we cannot control what locations are available. The key question here is: what do we do when none of those available locations seems likely to succeed? The correct strategic answer is that we do nothing. We wait.

5. *Progress means getting environment feedback not checking off to-do items.* If we can't find a location, we are stuck on dependent tasks such as doing a design, but we can work on independent tasks, such as investing other restaurant menus in the area and getting feedback from locals about what they want on a menu, but we must not take a poor location simply to keep to our schedule. We let dependent tasks, such as decorating the restaurant, wait.

6. *Each step is based upon the results of the last step.* For example, the location that we find determines our designs. If we find a good location, we want to see what kind of restaurants are already in that area before developing a design or our menu.

   7. Each step may be revisited based upon the results of the next step. We may get a good menu, but then have to change it because the ingredients and staff are available.

5.3 Reaction Time

Sun Tzu's five key methods on the use of speed in choosing actions.

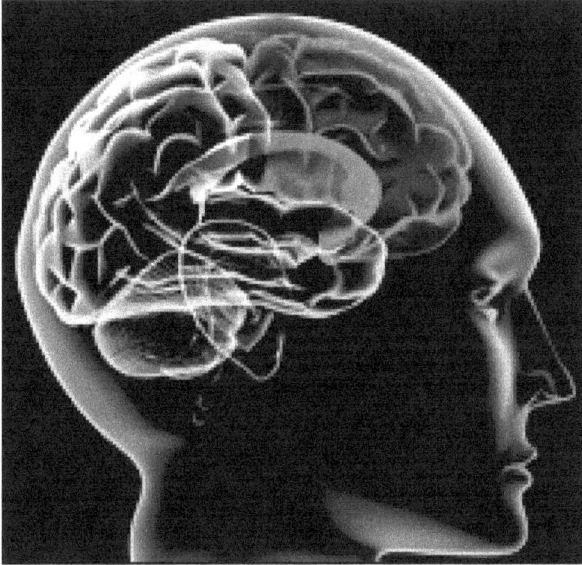

"Mastering speed is the essence of war."
Sun Tzu's The Art of War 12:2:16

"What comes first, the compass or the clock? Before one can truly manage time (the clock), it is important to know where you are going, what your priorities and goals are, in which direction you are headed (the compass). Where you are headed is more important than how fast you are going. Rather than always focusing on what's urgent, learn to focus on what is really important.

Anonymous

General Principle: Actions pursuing opportunities must be chosen quickly.

Situation:

When we choose how we want to pursue and opportunity, our first concern is minimizing mistakes. We don't want to endanger our current position or waste resources. It is natural to think that the best way to minimize mistakes in exploring opportunities is to go slowly and carefully. The problem is that slow reactions are almost always extremely costly in competitive environments. Of course, some forms of speed are extremely dangerous. For example, it is always dangerous to get heavily involved with a new opportunity before we have explored what is holds. Good strategy doesn't promote speed in the sense of a headlong rush.

Opportunity:

In choosing the best way to explore an opportunity, we cannot over estimate the value of speed. Sun Tzu wrote extensively about how and why speed is important. Acting and reacting quickly gives us a advantage in every strategic situation. The definition of a competitive situation is one in which we are compared to others (1.3.1 Competitive Comparison). The definition of a strategic situation is one in which we have to adjust to conditions and events in our environment (1.1.1 Position Dynamics). We are always compared by how quickly we respond. Our reaction time is often the difference between success and failure.

Key Methods:

The following key methods explain why actions that can be taken quickly are always preferable to slower reactions.

1. We can never start exploring an opportunity too soon. The faster we begin our exploration, the faster we can learn what an opportunity holds. As the saying goes, "He who hesitates is lost." This is especially true when it comes to taking advantage of opportunities. Natural forces in the environment open those windows of opportunity, but those openings are closed by other people filling them. The longer we delay in testing our new opportunities, the less likely we are to be successful in exploring and exploiting them (3.1.6 Time Limitations).

2. Any quick action increases our safety by decreasing conflict. If we react quickly to an opportunity, we get ahead of the competition. If we keep reacting quickly to what we discover, we can stay there. When we move quickly and with confidence, we discourage others from competing with us. This decreases the main risk in competition, the cost of conflict (3.1.3 Conflict Cost).

3. We *make fewer and less costly mistakes when we react quickly.* This is especially true if we have honed our strategic instincts through training and exercise. Competitive environments are too complex for us to consciously analyze. Our unconscious gut reactions process a great deal more information than our conscious mind can. If we are trained, we usually come to the right decisions automatically in high-pressure situations. We can easily over-think these if we take to much time. Focusing on unimportant details which we can understand rather than the big picture (2.5 The Big Picture)

4. Faster reaction times gain us more knowledge more quickly. This is not to say that, by acting quickly, we won't make mistakes. We will. However, fast reactions always have an advantage over delay. By acting quickly, even our mistakes quickly win us more knowledge. We can learn more from our mistakes than our successes. The mistakes that we make by hesitating are more expensive because they don't teach us a thing other than to act more quickly the next time (2.6 Knowledge Leverage).

5. Even a series of quick, safe failures dramatically increases our eventual probability of success. The issue of speed brings us face to face with the laws of probability. Our time is limited. Success in strategic environments is always a matter of probability rather than control. While strategic methods improve our chances of success, one of the ways it does that is simply by using speed to give us more tries. The more trials we get, the more likely our success becomes over time as long as none of our failures ends the process. This is why we must understand all the lessons in this section regarding minimizing our mistakes (4.0 Leveraging Probability).

Illustration:

Let us look at the example of going after a new position with a current employer.

1. We can never start exploring an opportunity too soon. If we want a promotion into a specific position, we are better off exploring that positions immediately, even before those openings are available, rather than later.

2. Quick action increases our safety by decreasing conflict. We should let the current position holders know of our interest in their job, and see if we can work with them to get them promoted. This opens the desired position sooner rather than later and we are positioned for it as the heir apparent. Done correctly, others may not even challenge us for the opening.

3. We make fewer and less costly mistakes when we react quickly. We can worry about threatening the current holders of the position, but we will know when we sound them out if they are threatened or flattered by the attention. We cannot guess at the situation without exploring it. If we worry about approaching people and delay, we will probably never do it.

4. Faster reaction times gain us more knowledge more quickly. Even if they are threatened and unwilling to help us, planning to keep their position for years, it is better to know that sooner rather than later.

5. Even a series of quick, safe failures dramatically increases our eventual probability of success. If one potential position proves to be a dead-end, we are better knowing that so we can look elsewhere rather than waiting. Even if we fail many times trying to find future openings and champions, we will certainly find them over time.

5.3.1 Speed and Quickness

Sun Tzu's seven key methods regarding the use of pace within a dynamic environment.

"You can fight a war for a long time or you can make your nation strong. You can't do both."
Sun Tzu's The Art of War 2:1:25

"In skating over thin ice our safety is our speed."
Ralph Waldo Emerson

General Principle: The best actions leverage both speed and quickness and recognize their difference.

Situation:

Not all our explorations of openings are going to be successful. Many, if not most, are going to fail. Our explorations fail because of two major reasons. First, the nature of the opening may not offer any real rewards. Second, we are too slow in finding out how to make that opportunity pay. Being too slow opens us up two types of failure 1) the competition beats us or 2) we run out of resources. The first problem comes from our limited knowledge. The second comes from our limited skill. While some skills may be beyond our capability, the most common cause of the second failure is the lack of focus on speed and quickness.

Opportunity:

We must focus on what we can control. Our resources are always limited (3.1.1 Resource Limitations). We cannot control it making some opportunities pay requires more than we can afford to invest. We can control our pace. Once we master the secret of speed and quickness, we can usually outpace our competitors. If we can fill an opportunity before others do, we dramatically increase our success rate (3.1.6 Time Limitations).

Key Methods:

Let us start with some clear definitions differentiating between speed and quickness.

1. Speed means directly closing the distance between our existing position and an open opportunity. Distance measures the space between positions. Distance exists both in physically space and in intellectual space. Covering physical space requires movement while covering intellectual space requires learning (4.4 Strategic Distance).

2. The best actions use speed to get through difficult ground with a minimum of risk. Tilted, fluid, and soft forms of ground open us up to certain forms of temporary problems. The longer we are on such ground, the larger our risk. This is especially true of soft ground, which gives out over time (4.3 Ground Forms).

3. Quickness is the ability to change directions rapidly. Quickness requires 1) seeing a situation, 2) making a decision, and 3) executing that decision. This is a general function of cycle time (1.8.3 Cycle Time).

4. Speed can work against quickness. Speed increases our inertia in a specific direction. Moving fast can make it harder to change direction. It can prevent us from seeing a situation and changing direction to adjust to it. Going faster and faster when we are going in the wrong direction creates more problems. Going in the right direction is always more important than our speed. We cannot afford to go so fast that we miss our turnoff (1.6.3 Shifting Priorities).

5. Quickness can work against speed. If we constantly worry whether we are going the right direction, we are going to end up going too slow. We must commit to our direction so we can build up speed. Mastering Sun Tzu's strategy gives us confidence in balancing speed against quickness, recognizing when the situation calls for speed and when for quickness (6.4.4 Open Situations). *The best actions use both speed and quickness to get ahead and stay ahead of competitors*. As with all strategic characteristics, both speed and quickness are evaluated only in comparison. We are only relatively faster or slower when compared with other competitors operating within our environment. We want to move faster toward the right solution than anyone else (1.3.1 Competitive Comparison).

6. If we cannot win a position on the basis of speed, we must use quickness. Some competitors are simply faster than we are. They get going first and at a good rate. We should recognize when we cannot catch up on speed alone. In those situations, we must focus on quickness. We must be prepared to change directions when events or the ground offer us an advantage (5.3 Reaction Time).

Illustration:

The critical difference between speed and quickness is most commonly recognized in the world of sports so I initially used baseball to illustrate them. However, in thinking about it, it seems that failures of intellectual speed and quickness are more common and more difficult to understand. Let us use selling as an example of an area where we have to develop intellectual speed and quickness.

1. Speed means directly closing the distance between our existing position and an open opportunity. In sales, the distance that we must close is a gap in knowledge, the gap between our product knowledge and our knowledge of the customer's needs. The more quickly we close that gap, the more sales we can make.

*2. **The best actions use speed to get through difficult ground with a minimum of risk**. The faster we learn about a given customer's needs, the more often we will avoid wasting time describing features and benefits that are meaningless to the sale.*

*3. **Quickness is the ability to change directions rapidly**. During the sales process, we eventually focus on a specific set of products and needs. We focus on a group of customers who have those needs. Quickness is our ability to see a better direction in dealing with a specific customer or meeting and change our focus.*

*4. **Speed can work against quickness.** If we have learned a lot about a particular set of customer problems, our inertia takes us in that direction. When a given customer situation calls for us to go in a new direction, we can easily miss the signs. Changing directions is often necessary because customers will see where we are going and put up barriers. Even if our direction is correct, we must quickly change direction to get around those barriers.*

*5. **Quickness can work against speed.** Customer situations are complex. We cannot learn everything about a customer's business. If we keep shifting directions like a puppy chasing chickens, the customer gets over-loaded with information and the sales process loses focus.*

*6. **The best actions use both speed and quickness to get ahead and stay ahead of competitors**. If we can out pace our competitors in identifying and addressing customer needs, quickly adapting to the unique aspect of every situation, we are going to be successful in selling. Our ability to do this speedily and quickly isn't a matter of simply being smarter than our competitors. It depends largely on having better mental models than they do so we can fill in the pieces more quickly.*

*7. **If we cannot win a position on the basis of speed, we must use quickness.** This is especially true when we are taking a customer away from a competitor. That competitor has a big lead over* us in terms of knowing that customer. We cannot close that gap by speed alone. We must use our quickness to take the sale in directions that put the competitions at a disadvantage.

5.3.2 Opportunity Windows

Sun Tzu's five key methods on the effect of speed upon opposition.

"Never waste an opportunity to defeat your enemy."
Sun Tzu's The Art of War 4:3:23

*I was seldom able to see an opportunity until it had
ceased to be one."*
Mark Twain

"Opportunities are never lost; they are taken by others."
Anonymous

General Principle: Opportunity duration is determined by the environment's speed and quickness.

Situation:

When we choose the way to explore an opportunity, we must ask ourselves how long that opportunity is likely to last. Opportunities only last long enough for the fastest and quickest competitors to take advantage of them, not one moment longer. One opportunity can disappear in a flash of insight during a single meeting. Other opportunities can linger on for decades, as a series of barriers are broached one by one. Fast actions waste resources in slow environments. Slower actions waste resources in faster environments.

Opportunity:

All opportunities are created by others (3.2.1 Environmental Dominance). All opportunities arise because an emptiness, a need, cries out to be filled (3.2.4 Emptiness and Fullness). Our opportunity starts with recognizing that need before others and seeing how our unique resources can fill it (3.4.2 Opportunity Fit). We can conserve our resources by avoiding opportunities that we are not in a position to fill. Speed and quickness affects both how rapidly opportunities emerge and how quickly those opportunities are satisfied. More opportunities emerge in fast environments, but more competitors are are prepared to take advantage of them there as well.

Key Methods:

When choosing the best way to explore an opportunity, we must consider the nature of our window of opportunity.

1. Generally, faster action is better than slower ones because all opportunities are temporary. All positions are temporary. The more temporary the positions that border the opening, the more temporary the opportunity itself. Faced-paced environments arise when everyone focuses on the temporary nature of their positions (1.1.1 Position Dynamics).

2. The pace of action must match the pace of the environment. Opportunities arise more rapidly in environments that welcome change. More competitive environments embrace change. Opportunities are stifled in environments that resist change. More regulated environments resist change. Our speed and quickness are always measured relative to the environment in which we work. We must always be faster than our competition, but we cannot get too far ahead of them. Too much speed within a slow environment will create friction. (1.3.1 Competitive Comparison).

3. *Quickness recognizes developing opportunities first.* In slower-paced environments, fewer people are open to seeing opportunities so windows of opportunity open more gradually. In fastpaced competitive environments, needs are more quickly recognized. In either case, the recognition of a problem is the firing of the starting gun at the beginning of a race. Quickness allows some people to get the jump on others (5.3 Reaction Time).

4. *Speed is required to secure an opportunity.* Again, this speed is relative. In a quick environment, we can be more reckless because success depends on speed more than anything else. In slower environments, we must aim for more measure progress because recklessness is heavily penalized. Whatever the environment, we take advantage of the opportunity by learning how to fill the openings more quickly than others (1.8.3 Cycle Time).

5. *The larger the organization, the larger window of opportunity it requires.* Larger organizations tend to identify opportunities more slowly and start moving more slowly because of the diseconomies of scale, especially slow reaction time. We would think that in the case of large opportunities, large organizations would be able to catch up to their smaller competitors because growth takes time. However, history shows that large organizations can only take advantage of opportunities that are very close to their current position because a fast organization can grow more rapidly than a large organization can move (3.4 Dis-Economies of Scale).

Illustration:

We can see this difference in comparing different environments, for example, the high-tech business environment with the federal government environment. High-tech is one of the environments most open to change because it is highly competitive. The federal government is one of the environments most resistant to change because it has no competition.

1. *Generally, faster action is better than slower ones because all opportunities are temporary.* In both the high-tech world and government, all opportunities are temporary. More of them are missed in government because of their pace.

2. *The pace of action must match the pace of the environment.* Try to act too quickly within a slow environment such as the federal government creates more problems than it solves. Unlike the hight-ech environment which embraces creative destruction, rash action creates potential disasters within the federal government because no government entity is allowed to fail. Witness Fanny Mae.

3. *Quickness recognizes developing opportunities first.* In the federal government, few people are open to seeing opportunities. Changes play out gradually over decades. In the world of high-tech, everyone is on the lookout for new opportunities because businesses and entire industry segments rise up and die out within a few years.

4. *Speed is required to secure an opportunity.* In high-tech, speed is measured in months. In the federal government, it is measured in years.

5. *The larger the organization, the larger window of opportunity it requires.* As organizations grow larger in high-tech, they find fewer and fewer opportunities so they are frequently outmoded and replaced. The US federal government, on the other hand, may have outgrown all possible opportunities except in size reduction.

5.3.3 Information Freshness

Sun Tzu's six key methods on the choosing actions based on freshness of information.

"You must have surviving spies capable of bringing you information at the right time."

Sun Tzu's The Art of War 13:4:10

"Life is made up of constant calls to action, and we seldom have time for more than hastily contrived answers."

Billings Learned Hand

" On the plains of hesitation bleach the bones of countless millions who, at the dawn of decision, sat down to wait, and waiting died."

Sam Ewing

General Principle: The best actions are based on the most recent information.

Situation:

A common strategic mistake is waiting to make the decision to act, hoping for better information. No matter how long we wait, our information is always incomplete. But, the longer we delay deciding on action, whatever correct information we have is likely to become outdated.

Opportunity:

The need for speed in choosing an action is based on our need to leverage information (2.6 Knowledge Leverage). We can make good decisions despite imperfect information (2.1.1 Information Limits). We can rely on situations constantly changing rather than battle against it (2.1.2 Leveraging Uncertainty). Once we act, we get immediate feedback about the nature of the situation, improving our actions in a constant cycle (1.8.2 The Adaptive Loop).

Key Methods:

In identifying the best actions, we must consider the following key methods relating to the nature of our information.

1. Timely action based on current information is always more likely to be successful than waiting for better information. All actions are experiments. Only by experimenting can we discover what is real. Information gathering through our information channels is a critical part of strategy, but it only goes so far. After identifying a high-probability opportunity, the best way to gather information about it is through action, not more information gathering (4.0 Leveraging Probability).

2. We must not act when conditions are changing so rapidly that our information is probably already outdated. Acting on the basis of outdated information is usually wasteful. It can also be dangerous, threatening our current position. When a fluid environment is going through dramatic shifts in climate, it is always better to wait then to act (4.3.2 Fluid Forms).

3. All actions must factor in the possibility that even the freshest information can be wrong. Recent information is not any more perfect than any other type of information. While fresh information is less likely to be outdated, we must, still choose actions that minimize our risks. When the information that we have requires action, we are always better off acting, rather than wasting time trying to get better information, but only if we choose actions that allow for our information being wrong (2.1.3 Strategic Deception.

4. New information is more likely to be correct when it is consistent with our situation awareness. We must always test new information against our sense of the big picture of our situation. If the information we get is consistent with our expectations, we can rely on it more heavily. New information that is inconsistent with our expectations can disprove our sense of the situation, but that information must be questioned (2.5 The Big Picture).

5. Even if action doesn't attain its desired goal, a quick response to events improves our subjective position. It demonstrates that we are decisive, improving our position in their eyes. Acting quickly is never acting rashly as long as we know how to experiment safely. By gauging our responses based on our fallibility, we demonstrate that we are not afraid of making mistakes if we can learn from them (5.0 Minimizing Mistakes).

6. We always get the advantage of surprise. We create events that others must respond to rather than passively react to events created by others (2.1.4 Surprise).

Illustration:

Let us illustrate these principles with an example from selling. What should we do if we hear that a customer has just gotten a very low price offer from a competitor.

1. Timely action based on current information is always more likely to be successful than waiting for better information. We must react instantly by contacting the customer rather than wait to see if we can get more specific information about the offer elsewhere.

2. We must not act when conditions are changing so rapidly that our information is probably already outdated. If offering low prices with many special conditions and restrictions is common in our industry, we should wait to see what the pricing really means before acting.

3. All actions must factor in the possibility that even the freshest information can be wrong. We must not react by trying to cut our prices. Our actions should be gauged to open up possibilities not close them down.

4. New information is more likely to be correct when it is consistent with our situation awareness. If this competitor normally tries to undercut prices, the news is probably correct. If this competitor seldom does, we should suspect it, but still react.

5. Even if action doesn't attain its desired goal, a quick response to events improves our subjective position. Our quick response will, at the minimum, show the customer that we are aware of what is happening and care about their business.

6. We always get the advantage of surprise. The response that we make should make price less of an issue rather than more of an issue. It should focus on questions of quality or long-term shared risk rather than price, forcing our competitors to adapt to us.

5.4 Minimizing Action

Sun Tzu's six key methods regarding minimizing waste, i.e. less is more.

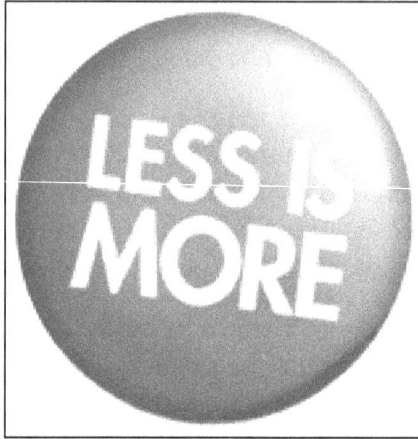

"Make good use of war.
Make the enemy's troops surrender.
You can do this fighting only minor battles."
                                    Sun Tzu's The Art of War 3:3:1-3

"Less is more."

                                    Ludwig Mies van der Rohe

General Principle: To do more with less we must focus on small areas of deep knowledge.

Situation:

Since Sun Tzu defines success in economic terms, we seek to do more with less. Every action we take or resource we use that we can eliminate is waste. In pursuing an opportunity, waste increases our risk of loss. If we try to improve our position by pursuing opportunity after opportunity by doing more and more different activities, our position grows more and more complex and waste multiplies. The result is that our position becomes more and more expensive and difficult to maintain.

Opportunity:

In choosing actions to safely pursue opportunities, we look for ways to eliminate waste. the strongest competitive actions are usually the simplest, most direct, and most economical. Strategic positioning is based on economical action (3.1 Strategic Economics). Since we cannot know the return from any new venture at the beginning, our first goal must be to control our costs. This means that the best strategy is doing less, not more. In choosing action, we must look to every new venture as a means of simplifying our current activities rather than making them more complicated.

Key Methods:

There is a science to Sun Tzu's approach to doing less that comes from choosing doing what is best not second-best.

1. We should choose activities that make our skills deeper rather than broader. When we focus our efforts on a smaller range of activities, we need in-depth knowledge, increasing the value of our capabilities. When we spread our efforts over an increasing range of different activities, we broaden our skills but decrease their value (1.5.2. Group Methods).

2. We should eliminate waste in using resources, movement, stockpiling, mistakes, and delay. These ideas are closely related to the seven mura of lean manufacturing, but they are also related directly to Sun Tzu's points of competitive vulnerability (9.2 Points of Vulnerability).

3. We should choose activities that simplify our external focus. Focus is a key source of power. If we pursue opportunities by becoming less and less focused, we weaken our position even as we seem to be expanding it. We want to broaden our external knowledge but focus that knowledge on smaller and smaller external regions. Spread-out positions and over-extended operations result from choosing to pursue activities by doing more and more instead of less and less (1.7.2 Goal Focus).

4. _Whenever possible, we want to grow by subtraction._ Doing one thing is easy. Doing many things is hard. A concentrated effort is powerful. A divided effort is weak. A well-defined target makes us successful. A vague target is hard to hit. Clear-cut goals keep us on track. Confused goals get us intro trouble. We must spend more time on activities that meet current demands while exploring new territory and spend less and less time on activities that do not take us into new areas. We should pursue opportunities as a way to escape from the lowest valued activities we are currently performing. To start a new venture, we need excess resources. These resources should be pulled away from our least profitable activities. We want to build our position up by focusing more narrowly on what we are already doing (3.3 Opportunity Resources):

5. _We can direct existing activities to take advantage of new opportunities._ One of the best ways to explore an opportunity is to use existing activities. We want to kill two birds with one stone. We can use existing skills for meeting our current commitments while exploring new territory at the same time. If two sets of activities are of equal value in maintaining our current position, we should choose those activities that allow us to move into new areas at the same time (2.6 Knowledge Leverage). For example, if a business sees a product line as a potential new opportunity, it is best to talk to existing customers in the regular course of business about its potential rather than seeking out new customers in new markets.

6. _We choose activities that decrease internal and external competition_. We must always remember that the most profitable moves are those that face the least competition. Competition can come from others, or it can come from competing internal activities. When choosing among potential ways of exploring an opportunity, we should pick the ones that decrease conflict because they will always be less expensive. Less conflicted activities are always more profitable ones (3.1.3 Conflict Cost).

Illustration:

The example that I always use for this in my lectures is the way that we built our software company, growing it an average of 40% a year from our profits alone for over a decade.

1. We should choose activities that make our skills deeper rather than broader. When we started our software company, we started as general consultants. Our most profitable jobs came from database development, so we slowly stopped doing other projects. By focusing on database projects, our business doubled. Then our most profitable projects were accounting related, so we focused on opportunities that were accounting related.

2. We should eliminate waste in using resources, movement, stockpiling, mistakes, and delay. Our least profitable activities were eliminated as waste since the resources that they used could be better applied to more profitable activities.

3. We should choose activities that simplify our external focus. We started selling any type of services to any type of company. By working more and more on accounting, we eventually developed a basic modifiable accounting package that other developers wanted to use and resell. Since selling software was more profitable than running projects, we gradually stopped our own projects and con-centrated on reseller sales. Then, the most profitable sales through those resellers started coming from larger system installations, with division of Fortune 500 companies. We began to concentrate our efforts on only those types of systems and resellers that could support them. Then we saw that our most profitable sales came from order processing companies. We stopped selling other types of accounting software and concentrated on companies with complex order-processing problems.

4. Whenever possible, we want to grow by subtraction. We became one of the Inc. 500 fastest growing companies in America not by doing more and more, but by doing less and less, at least in terms of our range of skills and customers. And we did it without any outside financing or borrowing money because we were always working at what was most profitable.

5. *We can direct existing activities to take advantage of new opportunities.* In making each of these transitions, we did not develop a new base of activities or skills. We simply make our knowledge deeper and narrowed our focus.

6. *We choose activities that decrease internal and external competition*. We ended up where we did, selling order-processing systems to sales-oriented divisions of large companies because there was less external competition for those projects and because they were consistent with the skill set in developing software.

5.4.1 Testing Value

Sun Tzu's five key methods on choosing actions to test for value.

"When you fall behind, you must catch up."
Sun Tzu, Art of War 7:1:11

"Simplicity and repose are the qualities that measure the true value of any work of art."
Frank Lloyd Wright,

General Principle: Choose the smallest action that tests the value of an opportunity.

Situation:

It is always a mistake to think that by spending more and more money, we can some how force an opportunity to produce the results that we want. Most of us realize that such an approach is simply throwing good money after bad. Only those expending other people's resources, i.e. those in government, can afford to continue programs that return little or no value to the investors.

Opportunity:

We cannot control the underlying, fundamental nature of an opportunity. The ultimate costs and benefits of controlling a given position are determined by the larger environment (3.2.1 Environmental Dominance). Our job is simply to choose the right positions. In improving our position, we therefore must seek to control what we can: our own expenditures. The more we minimize those expenditures, the more likely it is that a given move to a new position will be profitable (3.1.2 Strategic Profitability).

Key Methods:

Choosing the best activities must be constantly guided by the overarching and demanding economics of strategic profitability.

1. Our exploration of any opportunity must be designed as a test of our value assumptions. We pursue opportunities because we think they are likely to be valuable. We identify high probability opportunities by testing their surface characteristics from a distance. However, we cannot know the real value of that opportunity before exploring it directly. The principle of unpredictable value is the foundation of much strategy. Any assumptions we make about either the cost of benefits of a given opportunity are unproven. (3.1.5 Unpredictable Value).

2. We must limit our opportunity exploration to activities that directly determine whether or not an opportunity will pay. Doing less is better than doing more because doing less requires less investment. Fewer costs mathematically improve our likelihood of making a profitable move. At its root, all strategy is based on these simple economics (3.1 Strategic Economics).

3. If we can use cost-effective methods to explore opportunities, the more of them we can afford to explore. Since no given move is certain to be profitable, we must take a probabilistic approach, minimizing our failure and maximizing our successes. We limit our costs to focus our efforts on what really matters: making victory pay. In other words, we must find the shortest, simplest route possible to see if a given opportunity can pay for itself (1.8.4 Probabilistic Process).

4. *Only a precious few opportunities we pursue will prove to be as beneficial as we hope.* Even using the many strategic techniques for identifying high-probability opportunities, "high-probability" is a relative term. These opportunities are worth pursuing compared with what most people mistake for opportunities, but they are far from certain. Only by exploring many such opportunities do we make our success certain over time (4.0 Leveraging Probability).

5. *All tests of value must gauge our mission against our methods.* Our mission is what defines value. Our methods dictate our costs. In terms of costs,we always want to minimize our investment in exploring new territory. Small steps are not only safer but more powerful. However, smallness alone is not the measure for success. All exploration activities must identify the ways in which a new position can bring us closer to our goals (8.0 Winning Rewards).

Illustration:

For example, when I ran a software company, there were always many directions in which we could develop our software. We used Sun Tzu's techniques to identify which of those directions were best before we started a development project.

1. *Our exploration of any opportunity must be designed as a test of our value assumptions.* We would undertake only new development that we suspected that people would find valuable. Actually, we cheated a little. Most of our development projects were financed by customers so we knew that there was some value in the project.

2. *We must limit our opportunity exploration to activities that directly determine whether or not an opportunity will pay.* In designing that project, we asked ourselves only one question: what is the minimum product that we can sell? What is the minimum product for which a customer will pay?

3. If we can use cost-effective methods to explore opportunities, the more of them we can afford to explore. In our environment, we always saw the key limited resource as time to market. When we undertook speculative development products--those not funded by customers--we made sure that the people on the team understood the limits on risk. To make sure that newly developed product was the minimum product, we often set a deadline of three months to bring something to market. The team understood that if the product couldn't be passed off to sale in that span of time, it wouldn't get more time.

4. Only a precious few opportunities we pursue will prove to be as beneficial as we hope. Only the market, that is, the real world of our software customers, could tell us if we were on the right track or not. The sooner we could start asking people for money, the sooner we would know if we were on the right track or not. Many projects swallowed up our time, but they are forgotten. What we remember our successes because they became part of our position.

5. All tests of value must gauge our mission against our methods. No projects were approved unless they met the basic criteria of our mission: developing software that was modifiable-by-design, easily changed to adapt to a constantly changing environment.

5.4.2 Successful Mistakes

Six key methods regarding the advantages in learning from our mistakes.

"You can be stopped and yet recover the initiative.
You must use your days and months correctly.
If you are defeated, you can recover.
You must use the four seasons correctly."
Sun Tzu's The Art of War 5:2:7-10

Your future takes precedence over your past. Focus on
your future, rather than on the past."
Gary Ryan Blair

"Some of the best lessons we ever learn are learned
from past mistakes. The error of the past is the wisdom
and success of the future."
Dale E. Turner

General Principle: Choose actions to secure benefits rather than to prove past decisions correct.

Situation:

We come to each choice of action based on our past choices. When we explore what looks like an opportunity, we are often going to be disappointed by our initial choices. The challenge arises from our reactions to that disappointment. There are two opposite mistakes that we can make. On one hand, we can throw good money after bad, increasing the size of our loss by simply expanding on our initial efforts. On the other hand, we can abandon a good opportunity by failing to follow up after a poor initial choice. The question is how we find the right balance of persistence.

Opportunity:

We come to each choice of action based on our past choices. When we explore what looks like an opportunity, we are often going to be disappointed by our initial choices. The challenge arises from our reactions to that disappointment. There are two opposite mistakes that we can make. On one hand, we can throw good money after bad, increasing the size of our loss by simply expanding on our initial efforts. On the other hand, we can abandon a good opportunity by failing to follow up after a poor initial choice. The question is how we find the right balance of persistence.

Key Methods:

The key methods for choosing the appropriate actions to learn from our mistakes are:

1. Avoid investing in any actions to prove past decisions correct. The error of "throwing good money after bad" in economics is called the problem of sunk costs , investing more on the basis of unrecoverable past expenditures. It arises because people are loss averse. We have a stronger desire to avoid known losses than to make unknown gains. Without training, we are naturally sucked into investing more and more in opportunities, even when their value has been disproven. When we are responsible for a decision, we will tend to invest more to support that decision, even when we are disappointed in the results (1976 Staw and Fox) because we desire to prove our first decision correct. We can never make choices based upon past actions but on their future potential (4.1 Future Potential).

*2. **Loss aversion makes sense in defending positions but not in advancing them.*** There is a great deal of scientific research devoted to mapping the nature of loss aversion. As always, we see this natural bias as appropriate in the right framework. The research shows that we become more optimistic about an outcome after we have invested in it (1968 Knox and Inkster). This means that the more we invest, the more optimistic we become. This works for us when we are developing an existing position that is producing value. It works against us when trying to establish a new position where the value is unproven (1.9 Competition and Production).

*3. **The best action is never simply more of the same.*** Einstein defined insanity as repeating the same action expecting a different result. Since we are taught to think of size as an advantage, we can easily fall into thinking that our failure requires simply doing more. This is a dangerous approach in competitive environments where so much is unknown. Even if we can overcome the barriers that we discover with more resources, by investing more we decrease any likelihood of an opportunity being worth what it costs. The more time and resources we waste trying to make our original approach work, the fewer resources we have to find success along another path. The most important casualty of investing on the basis of sunk costs is the cost of wasting our other opportunities at finding success. (5.4 Minimizing Action).

*4. **We must base future actions on the knowledge gained from failure***. Every failure teaches us something about the boundaries of an opportunity and the barriers to exploiting it. The opening that defines an opportunity exists for a reason. Failure to exploit an opportunity tells us something about the nature of the opportunity. If we think of each move as an experiment, every action helps us because we learn more about the shape, size, and character of the opportunity. Because of the limits of information, we may know after a single action where the flaw lies, but we do know that there is a problem (4.5.2 Opportunity Barriers).

5. *We persist only as long as the opportunity meets the test of being our high-probability opening.* Our basis of choosing actions is always the same at every iteration of the adaptive loop: our probability of winning awards. After each failure, we measure what we have learned about the principles that define high-probability opportunities. If the opportunity still measures up as our best option, we must continue pursuing it (4.0 Leveraging Probability).

6. *We must choose actions that explore more of the opportunity's boundaries.* We must change our approach based upon what we have learned. Only by coming at an opportunity--AKA problem--from different angles do we learn its dimensions. If the opportunity is real, we will see progress in getting around the barriers that block the filling of an opportunity (4.5.2 Opportunity Barriers).

Illustration:

Let us look at the invention of the electric light bulb as an illustration of these principles. In that process, Thomas Alva Edison failed many times to find a filament that would work but continued on until he finally found a workable action. As Thomas Alva Edison said in his search for a good electric light filament, ***"I have not failed. I've just found 1,000 ways that won't work."***

The difference between Edison's repeated experiments and throwing good money after bad is that after all, Edison had no assurances that a viable filament existed. After testing a thousand materials that didn't work, he found himself making progress. Some materials worked better than others and, over time, he was able to identify the characteristics of the ideal material. He learned the dimensions of the opportunity space through his failures and, over time, was able to find materials that brought him closer and closer to his goal. In doing this, we seek to verify that the opening is real and that the problems it poses have an economical solution.

1. *Avoid investing in any actions to prove past decisions correct.* Over his career, Edison abandoned scores of ideas that did not prove out. He persisted with the electric light because he knew the need was real and the technology was conceptually correct.

*2. **Loss aversion makes sense in defending positions but not in advancing them.*** Edison's part in the <u>War of Currents</u> between Edison's direct current-based systems and Westinghouse's alternating currents was based mostly on Edison's loss aversion, but both sides had established companies.

*3. **The best action is never simply more of the same.*** To create the electric light, Edison tried over 3,000 different approaches to solving the problem of creating a usable light.

*4. **We must base future actions on the knowledge gained from failure***. As Thomas Alva Edison said in his search for a good electric light filament, ***"I have not failed. I've just found 1,000 ways that won't work."***

*5. **We persist only as long as the opportunity meets the test of being our high-probability opening.*** Some materials worked better than others. Making an element glow to create light was never an issue. The utility of electric light over gas lighting was never an issue. The issue was always one of functional design, how bright and how long.the light lasted.

*6. **We must choose actions that explore more of the opportunity's boundaries.*** Over time, Edison was able to identify the characteristics of the ideal material. He learned the dimensions of the opportunity space through his failures and eventually was able to find a couple of different materials that produced both enough light and lasted (persisted?) for a long time.

5.5 Focused Power

Sun Tzu's five key methods about size consideration in safe experimentation.

"Where you focus, you unite your forces."

Sun Tzu's The Art of War 6:4:3

"Simplicity means the achievement of maximum effect with minimum means."

Dr. Koichi Kawana

General Principle: Small steps are more certain and powerful.

Situation:

We cannot be successful if we fail to understand the critical relationship between safety and power. Most people confuse size with power. Large efforts seem more powerful even when they entail taking greater risks. This gets the formula for power exactly backwards. Properly understood, small moves are not only safer but more powerful. We cannot confuse a small, concentrated action with a weak, half-hearted one. The problem is that many of us do not know how to concentrate our actions to create power and minimize risk simultaneously.

Opportunity:

Powerful actions are concentrated. The safest way to test the potential of new opportunities is also the most powerful. The easiest way to minimize our risks is to limit the size of our experiments. The easiest way to create powerful actions is to concentrate our efforts in size. The most powerful actions are small, local, and quick.

Key Methods:

The following key methods define how we create focused power.

1. Competitive power comes from focused, concentrated activity. Power comes from focus and unity. Since size works against focus and unity, it creates weakness. The most powerful moves are those that concentrate intense, united effort in a small area of space and time. Diffusing our concentration of effort in larger groups, areas, and time period makes it less likely we will be successful (1.7 Competitive Power).

2. The more people involved, the less likely the move will be profitable. Number of people is the first dimension for measuring activity size. People have to be coordinated to pursue an opportunity. The larger that effort, the more costly the action will be. Large groups are simply more difficult to work with in exploring new opportunities. Costs often grows logarithmically as more and more people get directly involved in the project (5.5.1 Force Size).

3. The greater the distance to be covered, the less likely the move will be profitable. Strategic distance is the second dimension measuring the size of an action. Long moves require more resources so they are less likely to be profitable. In using Warrior's Playbook, we measure distance both in physical space and mental space. This means "distance" also measures the amount of information to be learned to complete a move. A local move requires us to cover territory that we already know (5.5.2 Distance Limitations).

4. *The greater the time it takes to get results, the less likely the move will be profitable.* The feedback loop is the circulatory system of strategy. Without feedback, we have nothing. With sluggish feedback, we must spend more time going in a direction before finding if we are off course or not. One of the easiest ways to control costs is to set deadlines for exploration activities to produce results (5.5.3 Evaluation Deadlines).

5. *All three dimensions of activity also affect speed.* Larger forces are slower; longer distances take more time, and slower feedback loops are, well...slower. The time value of resources means that longer moves are more expensive and therefore less likely to be profitable. Smaller actions measured in these three dimensions are always better. One of the ways we do this is to gravitate toward actions that are the smallest possible steps in these three dimensions (5.3 Reaction Time).

Illustration:

Let us think about these lessons from the perspective of developing a new product. We will use SOSI's philosophy of developing strategic training games for download.

1. *Competitive power comes from focused, concentrated activity.* We initially develop our games as manual games with playing cards, boards, and pieces. They are developed as downloads PDFs where the users "manufacture" the game by printing it. This takes much less time than our manufacturing the game and, given current technology, than developing them as a computer game, even though we would prefer that form long-term.

2. *The more people involved, the less likely the move will be profitable.* Games, like books, are developed by one person. When we have tried to develop games in groups, it just leads to endless discussion instead of a product.

3. *The greater the distance to be covered, the less likely the move will be profitable.* There are a lot of principles in strategy. A game that teaches many of them would create a lot of distance in the game. Such a game would be difficult to design and to learn to play. We limit our games to teaching just a handful of strategic principles. This makes our games easier to learn. To further reduce the learning distance, our games are either based on existing games or designed to be self-explanatory.

4. The greater the time it takes to get results, the less likely the move will be profitable. We develop our initial versions around the idea that the game can be extended over time by the addition of new rules over time. This allows us to easily improve the game and extend its lesson content, based on the interest that we get from our customers.

5. All three dimensions of activity also affect speed. We should be able to upgrade existing games several times a year while adding new games. More importantly, as the games get more refined and popular, we can convert them into a digital form. Ideally as the technology for creating portable phone apps matures and prices come down.

5.5.1 Force Size

Sun Tzu's eight key methods about limiting the size of force in an advance.

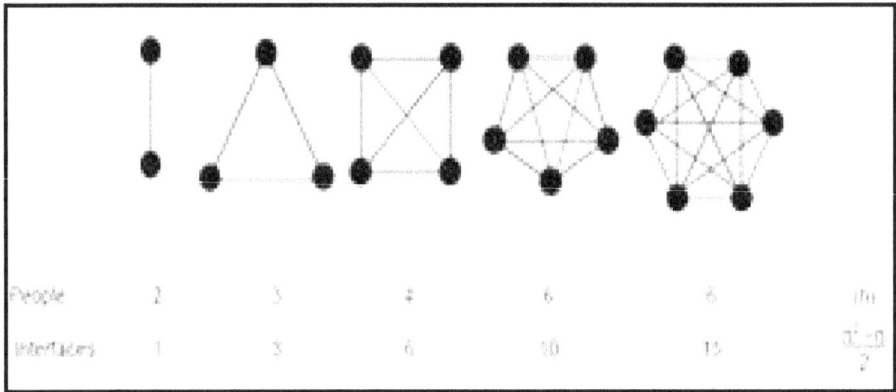

People	2	3	4	6	8	10
Interfaces	1	3	6	10	15	$\frac{n\cdot(n-1)}{2}$

> *"Using a huge army in battle success is very expensive. Long delays create a dull army and sharp defeats."*
>   Sun Tzu The Art of War 2:1:12

> *"Force is all-conquering, but its victories are short-lived."*
>
>   Abraham Lincoln

General Principle: To explore opportunities, choose actions that require a minimum of force.

Situation:

While there are competitive situations where we must use all of our resources to survive, choosing our actions for exploring opportunities is never one of them. Exploring new opportunities requires a minimum rather than maximum use of force. When we constantly invest too much in each opportunity, we soon find ourselves out of resources. Large forces take more time to organize and they always move slower since, to stay together, they are tied to the pace of their slowest component.

Opportunity:

We learn to separate the concept of "force" and "strength" from that of "power." Strategic power comes from unity and focus (1.7 Competitive Power). Strategic strength arises when we target an opposing weakness (3.5 Strength and Weakness). Both depend on leveraging the situation. Force, on the other hand, is simply using an abundance of resources to overpower a challenge or problem.

Key Methods:

These are the key methods defining the use of strategic force.

1. Competitive power comes from focused, concentrated activity. Po*Force is a matter of the size of effort.* When we talk about the size of a strategic force, we are talking about the size of the investment we make in a move. These investments are made in whatever resources are appropriate to the situation: manpower, money, reputation, relationships, emotion, and so on (3.3 Opportunity Resources).

2. Force is successful at too great a cost. This is based on the simple economics of opportunity. We use minimum force in exploring opportunities to reduce our costs. The bigger the investment we make, the more difficult it is for any opportunity to return more benefits than its costs (3.1 Strategic Economics).

3. The use of force limits the opportunities that we can explore. Our resources are always limited. The more force we use, the fewer opportunities we can afford to explore. Too much use of force eventually depletes the resources that we need to defend our existing position (3.1.1 Resource Limitations).

4. Even with force, most opportunities produce limited returns. We can hope each opportunity will provide a huge step forward, but we know that most will disappoint us. Most advances that we make in our position are small. Often all we gain from our efforts is a better picture of our situations (3.1.5 Unpredictable Value).

5. *The use of force alone often generates an escalation of opposing force*. This is Newton's Third Law: "To every action there is an equal and opposite reaction." In competitive situations, the use of force tends to create wars of attrition where both sides expend resources instead of leveraging strategy (2.3.1 Action and Reaction).

6. *Small advances can be profitable if we limit our use of force.* Each small advances can be profitable if we don't risk too much on any one of them. Over time, the accumulation of small advances dramatically improve our position over time. The small moves ideally put us in the right position at the right time to catch a major wave of climate change, but even if we are never that fortunate, our progress is constant and secure (3.1.2 Strategic Profitability).

7. *Amassing and using a large force take too much time.* The larger the force we use, the slower it takes us to respond to an opportunity. The more difficult it is to move that force, since all groups are limited by their slowest member. Since all opportunities are limited in time, the larger the force involved, the more likely the opportunity is to get away from us (3.1.6 Time Limitations).

8. *Even potentially large opportunities are better tested by small, exploratory forces.* These forces can gather information and discover the lay of the land much more quickly and efficiently than large forces. While we may need much more resources to fill a position, we have to remember that exploring a position is not the same as developing it. If an opportunity proves to have a very large potential, we will have time to increase the size of force. Ideally, we let the opportunity itself pay for its own development (8.2 Making Claims).

Illustration:

Using large forces is a lot like going "all in" in Texas Hold'em. Let's use that idea as our example.

1. Force is a matter of the size of effort. Going "all in" is the maximum effort, what Sun Tzu calls a "fight," that is, investing everything in the effort.

2. Force is successful at too great a cost. As they say, going "all in" works every time but the last one.

3. The use of force limits the opportunities that we can explore. If we use this tool all the time, it is just a matter of time until we run into a hand that beats us.

4. Even with force, most opportunities produce limited returns. All-In usually scares off opponents from calling when the pot is small, but then we can only win a small amount. When we eventually get unlucky and an opponent has a strong hand, possibly even the "nuts," we will almost always get called and likely lose everything for a usually small potential gain. The larger the pot-- and the more desperate the opponent--the more likely it is that we will be called. Even when we go into the All-In with a strong hand, often winning is simply a matter of luck, since in any given show-down, the odds can go against us. Eventually our straight will meet another flush.

5. The use of force alone often generates an escalation of opposing force. The more often a player uses the All-In, the more likely it is that he will get called because others will assume he is frequently bluffing.

6. Small advances can be profits if we limit our use of force. We do not have to go All-In to get other players to drop out. A series of small raises often looks more threatening because it seems to invite a call.

7. Amassing and using a large force take too much time. A large stack takes a great deal of time to accumulate but can be lost in a single moment with the "All-In". It takes even longer if we are gambling with our earnings in the normal business of the real world, outside of the poker table. y.

8. *Even potentially large opportunities are better tested by small, exploratory forces.* Since the rules of Hold-em eventually force an All-In, it is best to set up the All-in by a history of more conservative betting. Even within a given hand, the play works best after escalating from a series of smaller bets that test an opponent's resolve and build up potential winnings if the All-in forces the opponent out.

5.5.2 Distance Limitations

Sun Tzu's eight key methods on the use of short steps to reach distant goals.

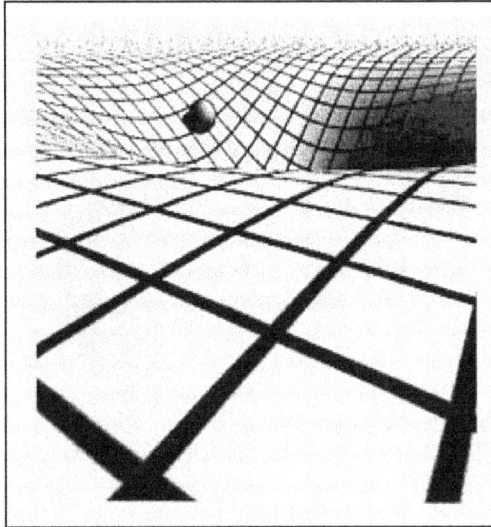

"Stay close to home to await the distant enemy."
Sun Tzu's The Art of War 7:5:13

"Whoever wants to reach a distant goal must take small steps."
Saul Bellow

General Principle: When exploring opportunities, choose actions that minimize the distance covered.

Situation:

The danger here is the romance of distance. The grass always seems greener somewhere else. The problem is that the further we travel, the bigger our investment in effort and time. The bigger our investment, the more costly it is for us to explore opportunities. The more costly exploration is, the less of it we can afford to do and the less we will profit in general from advancing our position.

Opportunity:

This principle of using short moves is based on the simple economics of exploring opportunities (3.1 Strategic Economics). To identify the best opportunities, we look for openings that are close to home (4.4 Strategic Distance). In choosing the best actions to explore any opportunity, we use our closeness to the situations to our advantage. This means picking actions that minimize both the physical distance (4.4.1 Physical Distance) and the intellectual distance (4.4.2 Intellectual Distance) that we must travel. If our move to a new position requires others to move toward us, we must also minimize the distance that they have to cover as well.

Key Methods:

These are the key methods defining the use of strategic force over distance.

1. Short steps are more powerful. This means we not only look for opportunities that are nearby, but we also move toward those opportunities by the shortest possible <u>open</u> route. The longer the route we choose, the more chances there are that we will encounter unforeseen problems. The ideal moves forward are always local ones. We must learn to prefer opportunities that are physically close to where we are now and intellectually close to what we already know (<u>4.4 Strategic Distance</u>).

2. We also want to shorten the distance our supporters must cover. While we tend to talk about exploring opportunities in terms of how far we must go, it is always the reaction of others that determines our success or failure. If we want the support of others, we must find ways to shorten their route, making it easier for them to do so. The closer we can get to them, the easier it is for them to support us (<u>2.3.1 Action and Reaction</u>).

3. Minimizing distance means simplifying our moves. In terms of testing the ground for value, simple tests are always better than more complicated ones. They are easier to execute and their results are easier to understand. While it is true that there are no shortcuts to success, we should always be looking for shortcuts when it comes to exploring opportunities. It is easier to test ground that we mostly understand rather than ground that is more foreign to us. (5.4.1 Testing Value).

4. The shortest route is that most in line with our current mission. Our mission sets the direction. While conditions and the nature of the ground can make a detour the shortest route, our mission is the compass that guides us (1.6 Mission Values)

5. The shortest route follows the dominant trends of climate. Change can bring the future to us so that we don't have to go to it. Having the wind at our backs makes every journey shorter ((1.4.1 Climate Shift).

6. The shortest route goes around obvious barriers. Going around barriers is usually easier than going over them. We do not want to fight gravity any more than we want to fight the wind (4.5.2 Opportunity Barriers).

7. The shortest route demands decisions that are easier to make. If a decision is difficult to make the problem is knowledge and information. Difficult decisions are a clear sign of intellectual distance (1.5.1 Command Leadership).

8. The shortest route utlizes skills that we already have. This is the methods aspect of intellectual distance. The more skills we must master or the more systems we must develop, the longer and less favorable the route (4.4.2 Intellectual Distance)

Illustration:

Let us explain these principles using the illustration of developing a new product.

1. Short steps are more powerful. A small simple product is better than a large complex one.

*2. **We also want to shorten the distance our supporters must cover.*** An inexpensive, easy-to-buy, and easy to use product is better than an expensive and difficult one.

*3. **Minimizing distance means simplifying our moves.*** Before developing a more sophisticated version, we should create a simpler prototype.

*4. **The shortest route is that most in line with our current mission**.* Make sure that the product unifies and focuses the business rather than spreading it out.

*5. **The shortest route follows the dominant trends of climate**.* The product should utilize popular technologies and relate to what is new and exciting.

*6. **The shortest route goes around obvious barriers.*** If there are obvious difficulties implementing a given feature, find an alternative feature that addresses the problem in a different way.

*7. **The shortest route demands decisions that are easier to make**.* If it is difficult to choose one feature at the expense of another, compromise.

*8. **The shortest route utilizes skills that we already have**.* We develop for existing "off-the-shelf" assembly and distribution methods rather than ones that have to be developed from scratch.

5.5.3 Evaluation Deadlines

Sun Tzu's six key methods for setting deadlines for evaluating progress.

Each day passes quickly.
A month can decide your failure or success.
　　　　　　　　　Sun Tzu's The Art of War 6:8:14-15

"A goal is a dream with a deadline."

Napoleon Hill

General Principle: When exploring opportunities, set the quickest possible deadlines for evaluating progress.

Situation:

While small amounts of force and moving short distances can save time, saving time alone is not our goal. Using a small amount of force and moving short distances has advantages in safety and power, but such moves can be too small to have any effect. A move can have so little force that it creates no results. A move can cover so little distance that we do not gain any new perspective on an opportunity. In choosing actions to take advantage of an opportunity, we can waste time both by doing too much and by doing too little.

Opportunity:

Setting deadlines for evaluation is a powerful tool for focusing the power of our competitive moves. When pursuing opportunities, we must choose actions that can be evaluated quickly. The key to success is getting feedback (1.8.3 Cycle Time). Using the smallest amount of force is quicker than assembling and organizing large ones. The smaller our forces the quicker they move but the action uses time effectively only when it gets feedback (5.5.1 Force Size). The closer our target, the sooner the move is completed but completing a move means getting actionable information (5.5.2 Distance Limitations). This means that we choose actions that have a stopping point for evaluation.

Key Methods:

The following key methods describe the value of an aggressive approach to setting deadlines.

1. Since each action has an end, it allows us to set a deadline for its completion. Taking an action on an opportunity is a discrete, time-limited event. Unlike analysis and observation, which are continuous processes, each competitive move to explore an opportunity should have a beginning, middle, and an end. To act on an opportunity, we have to physically do something, not just think about doing something. (5.4 Minimizing Action).

2. *An evaluation deadline isn't the end of exploration, but a stopping point for evaluating our progress.* In picking the right ways to The faster that we can get feedback about our success or failure in exploring an opportunity, the more successful we will be over time. Exploration is best performed in a series of stages, where each stage justifies the next (5.2 Opportunity Exploration).

3. *We choose actions that can be executed rapidly and evaluated quickly so we can adapt to what we learn.* This learning allows us to better explore an opportunity. This rule is the practical implementation of the principles teaching the importance of fast reaction times, speed, quickness, and short cycle times in executing strategy (5.3 Reaction Time).

4. *Deadlines not only help us keep in touch with our environment, they often improve our performance.* The most successful actions in competitive environments are those which we begin immediately and complete quickly. The more time we take, the less likely we are to be successful. Unlike production, where adding time can improve control and quality, competition never benefits from slowing down the process. They specifically help us avoid project creep where we get caught up in the infinite loops that are so common in competitive environments (2.3.5 Infinite Loops).

5. *Setting aggressive deadlines forces us to learn the maximum pace of our environment.* As we discussed in predicting the duration of opportunity windows, different environments work at different paces. An aggressive deadline is one that is unusually short for the environment in which we work, but not so short that results are impossible given the pace of the environment (5.3.2 Opportunity Windows).

6. *Wildly optimistic deadlines are better for choosing actions than more practical ones.* When we first started setting deadlines in a new competitive arena, our expectations for seeing results will often prove to be wildly optimistic given the pace of the environment. Though we may initially miss most deadlines in terms of getting feedback from our environment, through the practice of setting them, we eventually learn how to take action that gets the fastest possible feedback. The practice of setting deadlines is itself an adaptive loop where we learn how to do it better and better over time. One of the reasons we stay close to home is so we can learn realistic feedback times (1.8.2 The Adaptive Loop).

Illustration:

Let us use examples from businesses in which I have personally worked, the software industry, publishing, and developing on-line content.

1. Since each action has an end, it allows us to set a deadline for its completion. Developing a software product, writing and publishing a book, and creating on-line content are all discrete events for which we can set deadlines.

2. An evaluation deadline isn't the end of exploration, but a stopping point for evaluating our progress. Software has multiple versions, books multiple editions, and web content is continually updated. Within each of these processes, there are a series of smaller deadlines where we can evaluate progress.

3. We choose actions that can be executed rapidly and evaluated quickly so we can adapt to what we learn. We can only know how well a software product, a book, or web contents will be received by releasing it. But we can judge how easily more complicated products such as software or books are coming together at earlier stages. If a software product or a book runs into problems, we want to learn it as soon as possible.

4. Deadlines not only help us keep in touch with our environment, they often improve our performance. Software development is especially prone to mission creep because there are an infinite number of features that might be valuable, but writers can also suffer writer's block. The best cure for such blocks is the need to get something out at a given deadline.

*5. Setting aggressive deadlines forces us to learn the maximum pace of our environment. T*here is a huge difference between the pace in the software industry and the pace in the book publishing business. In software, we could release new products whenever we wanted, coming up with new ideas and selling them as soon as we could put together a demonstration to see if they were financially viable. However, in the book publishing business, the major book chains require six months notice and it usually requires a year of cycle time to get real feedback to learn how well a book is selling. Of course, the web-environment is both faster, because we can bring out new content continuously, but also it is more patient, since old material is always new to those who are just discovering it.

6. Wildly optimistic deadlines are better for choosing actions than more practical ones. In software development, our standard for new products was three months from assigning a developer (usually only one) to a version our salespeople could demonstrate. In books, our standard deadline from start to sending to the printer was less than ten weeks, even though the releases were planned a year ahead of time. In web content, we have committed to producing new Principle a Day articles every day and new game download products every month.

5.6 Defensive Advances

Sun Tzu's six key methods on balancing defending and advancing positions.

"*Defend when you have insufficient strength.
Attack when you have a surplus of strength.*"
Sun Tzu's The Art of War 4:2:5-6

"*The best defense is a good offense.*"
Carl von Clausewitz

General Principle: Defend on the basis of weaknesses, advance on strength, and do both when possible.

Situation:

It is commonly said that the best defense is a good offense, but this idea can easily be misunderstood. Defense means protecting our ability to exploit our position. It is the opposite of offense, which means exploring new opportunities for advancing our position. If we are always exploring opportunities and never exploiting them, we get no advantage from exploration. We can get into serious trouble when we do not clearly understand how defending positions relates to advancing them.

Opportunity:

Before committing to an action to explore an opportunity, we must balance defense against advance. We usually defend out of weakness and advance out of strength, with defense having the priority. The best actions, however, can sometimes do both at once. Our opportunity is to clearly connect exploring new positions with exploiting our existing position.

Key Methods:

The following key methods describe how we balance defending and advancing positions and how we can occasionally do both at once.

1. Exploiting an existing position requires defending that position. All our resources come from our existing position. If we lose any part of our position, we have fewer resources, making it more difficult to find opportunities to advance. Defense requires a special set of skills. Those skills start with recognizing our vulnerabilities and knowing how to defend them (9.0 Understanding Vulnerability).

2. The balance between defense and advance depends on the stability of our current position. Correctly understood, all advances are somewhat defensive because our existing position is only temporary, naturally decaying over time. We must therefore advance our position at some point in order to keep it from getting worse over time. Normally, most positions are fairly stable, decaying slowly, allowing us plenty of time to advance our position. However, when our current position is collapsing due to environmental conditions beyond our control, we must divert resources from defense to advance (1.1.1 Position Dynamics).

3. We normally defend existing positions based on our weaknesses. If we have vulnerabilities, our resources must first be spent creating a defense. If we leave others no openings, they are discouraged from attacking us and defending our existing position is easy. However, openings are a matter of opinion as well as fact. If people perceive openings, we can be attacked even if that perception is unjustified. If we leave openings undefended, real or imaginary, an attack by others is inevitable. Our first responsibility is therefore always to shore up our vulnerabilities (5.6.1 Defense Priority).

4. We must avoid actions exploring opportunities that expose our weaknesses. We gain credibility by our incumbency, that is, by our holding our current position. People assume that we have our position for good reasons, even without knowing us. We can maintain their good opinion if we don't violate this assumption. When we pursue opportunities with actions that highlight our weaknesses, we call our current position into question, making it more vulnerable instead of less so (1.2 Subobjective Positions).

5. We advance by choosing actions that emphasize our strengths. Opportunities are openings that we can fill, needs we can satisfy, and weaknesses that are complemented by our strengths. The excess resources that we use to pursue opportunities are an excess of strength. We cannot win a better position unless we demonstrate our abilities. We can only do this by pursuing opportunities in a way that highlight our strengths. Any demonstration of strength improves an existing position by justifying people's confidence in us (3.4.2 Opportunity Fit).

6. The gap between reality and perception allows us to both defend and advance positions at the same time. Though we defend on the basis of weakness and advance on the basis of strength, we can accomplish both at once when people perceive a weakness where there is really strength. By choosing activities that defy people's expectations, we both strengthen our existing position while advancing it. The best actions for pursuing opportunities are those that utilize resources that others did not realize we had (3.6 Leveraging Subjectivity , 5.4 Minimizing Action).

Illustration:

Let us look at these principles using the simple illustration of defending and advancing a job position.

1. Exploiting an existing position requires defending that position. We cannot get a promotion if people do not think we are doing a good job at our current position.

2. The balance between defense and advance depends on the stability of our current position. If our current employer is failing, we have to use our current position to find a new position with a different employer.

3. We normally defend existing positions based on our weaknesses. If we want to bolster up our current position, we must focus on erasing the doubts that people have about our abilities.

4. We must avoid actions exploring opportunities that expose our weaknesses. If we look for a change of position within a company because we are failing at our current job, we further undermine our existing position.

5. We advance by choosing actions that emphasize our strengths. Normally, we look to expand our responsibilities and authority in areas where we have had success.

6. The gap between reality and perception allows us to both defend and advance positions at the same time. If our employers have made bad judgments about our capabilities in a given area, we should dispel those opinions by seeking a promotion based upon our strengths in those areas of presumed weakness. We use the opportunity to make our case and extol our virtues that others are missing. Even if we do not win the new position, we shore up the vulnerabilities affecting our current position.

5.6.1 Defense Priority

Seven key methods regarding why defense has first claim on our resources.

*"You can divide the ground and yet defend it.
Don't give the enemy anything to win."*
Sun Tzu's The Art of War 6:3:14-15

"First, do no harm. (Primum nil nocere.)"
Auguste François Chomel

General Principle: Choose only actions that strengthen rather than risk a current position.

Situation:

We explore opportunities to identify how to advance our position. These explorations are experiments. We never know if they will work or not. To experiment safely, we must always consider the effect of our actions on our current position. The problem is that certain types of actions are incompatible with certain types of positions. We endanger our position when we take actions without considering their effect on our position.

Opportunity:

The basis of all opportunity is in preserving existing positions until our advances are successful (1.1.2 Defending Positions). In attempting to advance our position, we change it, even if we are merely extending our existing position in a small way. This is true whether the transition is successfully or not. Any move temporarily decreases our resources so we cannot move when we don't have resources needed for defense (3.3 Opportunity Resources). We avoid danger by putting our first priority on defense, foreseeing any actions potentially deleterious effects on our existing position.

Key Methods:

The key methods describing the logic and method for putting defense first are as follows.

1. Every position has weaknesses. We must choose actions that ideally alleviate those weaknesses rather than exacerbate them. We pick actions that leverage our current strengths. Indeed, our strengths cannot help but create weaknesses because strength and weakness are complementary opposites, two sides of the same underlying condition (3.5 Strength and Weakness). Going back to our rock climbing example, we must pick new holds that make our existing hold stronger. We must *never* try for new untested holds that pull us away from our current position.

2. Weakness is not the same as vulnerability. Simply because we have weaknesses doesn't mean that our existing position is vulnerable to attack. A vulnerability is an opening that allows opponent can undermine a key resources of our position. Vulnerabilities arise when we leave key resources needed to maintain our position undefended (9.0 Understanding Vulnerability).

3. Actions pursuing opportunities should never create key vulnerabilities. This means that they should never endanger the five key points of vulnerability--personnel, short and long-term resources, transportation/communication, and organization. Before committing to any action, we must make sure that we are not opening these five areas to attack (9.2 Points of Vulnerability).

4. Actions pursuing opportunities should never move against the form of our current position. While we normally use "form" as a way of evaluating potential opportunities, we must also consider the form of our current position. We should not choose actions that violate the gravity, current, and stability of our current position (4.3 Opportunity Forms).

5. Actions pursuing opportunities must not over-extend our position's area. There is a point at which a position becomes too spread-out to defend. Before pursuing some opportunities, we must eliminate other areas of activity to prevent this (4.6.1 Spread-Out Conditions).

6. Actions pursuing opportunities must not erode barriers protecting our position. If our actions damage some of the barriers of entry currently protecting our position, we should not undertake them. We must find actions that protect the existing barriers that protect us (4.6.4 Wide-Open Conditions).

7. Actions pursuing opportunities must consider our current position's holding power. There is a reason why Sun Tzu described the characteristics of holding power as dangers. Moving from a fixed position means that we are giving up a local peak position, which is seldom a good decision. Moves from sensitive position are risky because they mean giving up our existing position and not returning to it (4.6.5 Fixed Conditions , 4.6.6 Sensitive Conditions).

Illustration:

We can compare advancing a position to rock climbing. We move up one hold at a time. We must use our current position to support our weight while we find a new hold that will support us. We transfer gradually from an existing hold to the new one. We reach out and test several holds to find the one that works best.

1. Every position has weaknesses. In climbing a mountain, we cannot stay in any position forever. We must move up or down.

2. Weakness is not the same as vulnerability. Just because each hold is temporary, it doesn't mean that it is a weak hold. It cannot give way too soon.

3. Actions pursuing opportunities should never create key vulnerabilities. We must pick new holds that make our existing hold stronger. We must *never* try for new untested holds that pull us away from our current position.

4. Actions pursuing opportunities should never move against the form of our current position. If the angle of our existing position utilizes gravity, it holds us down. We cannot choose a new hold with an angle that pulls us away from that downward pressure.

5. Actions pursuing opportunities must not over-extend our position's area. Our arms and legs can only reach so far. Overreaching, using holds that are too far apart makes us weaker and can easily get us stuck or dislodged.

6. Actions pursuing opportunities must not erode barriers protecting our position's area. If a outcropping is blocking the wind, we do not want to take a hold that suddenly exposes us to it.

7. Actions pursuing opportunities must consider our current position's holding power. If we have to jump to a new hold, we must be absolutely, positively certain that it will take our weight.

5.6.2 Acting Now

Sun Tzu's eight key methods on acting on opportunities immediately.

"You must know the time of battle."
Sun Tzu's The Art of War 6:6:2

"So never lose an opportunity of urging a practical beginning, however small, for it is wonderful how often in such matters the mustard-seed germinates and roots itself."
Florence Nightingale

"Procrastination is the fear of success. People procrastinate because they are afraid of the success that they know will result if they move ahead now. Because success is heavy, carries a responsibility with it, it is

much easier to procrastinate and live on the 'someday I'll' philosophy."

Denis Waitley

"Procrastination is, hands down, our favorite form of self-sabotage."

Alyce P. Cornyn-Selby

General Principle: Given an opportunity, excess resources, and a viable action, we must act immediately to explore opportunities.

Situation:

Though there are many principles for choosing the best action, we must internalize those principles so that our decision for action can become automatic and instantaneous. This may seem impossible because there are such a large number of interconnected principles that guide us to choose both the best opportunities to pursue and the best action to pursue them. The reason that most of us are not more successful is simply because we don't have the right mental models and that lack creates a commonplace failure to act on our opportunities.

Opportunity:

Though we can describe the principles of strategy in a list of principles, these principles are not a to-do list, but a description of a series of related mental models. We train our instincts to instantly gravitate toward the best possible actions so we can take immediate action. Our mental models work on a subconscious level to process a complex array of conditions that defy the linear reasoning that we have been taught to use consciously. Our goal is not choosing a perfect action eventually but a viable action instantly. Our instant actions are seldom brilliant, exciting, or impressive. They usually seem insignificant and dull. What makes this series of little, small actions so powerful is our insistence on doing them now so that their effects accumulate quickly over time.

Key Methods:

To master the habit and power of acting instantly, we must master the following:

1. We must develop a prejudice toward taking immediate action to explore opportunities. Immediate actions requires only three ingredients 1) any opportunity, any opening, no matter how small 2) excess resources of time, money, etc., 3) any small action that tests that opportunity with those resources. When the three ingredients are present, our instinctual response should be to use them (4.0 Leveraging Probability).

2. We must internalize the mental models for choosing opportunities and actions. This means that we must practice them until they become second nature. Though there are many different principles, these mental models describe a few underlying related concepts from a variety of perspectives. We link principles to each other to train minds in the general concepts rather than specifics of terminology or condition (2.2.2 Mental Models).

3. As long as an action does not damage our existing position, we should try it. If it *does* damage our current position, we should reject it so we can come to an action that doesn't hurt our position (5.6.1 Defense Priority).

4. A single action will not likely make a difference, but a pattern of action will. The chances are that any one action won't seem to make a huge difference in our lives, at least not at first. Exploration takes time. Most of these actions will amount to little or nothing. However, over time, if we are constantly exploring opportunities, we cannot help but be successful. Patterns of success breed more successes while patterns of failure to act breed more failures. If we continue to act on them, we will continually find new opportunities to advance our position in small ways until we end up making huge progress (5.2 Opportunity Exploration).

5. Choosing small actions make acting now much easier. The best action is *never* a major commitment of effort. By definition, it is small, local, and quick. We do not make instant decisions about undertaking campaigns to get around barriers but about the small focused efforts that work best in pursuing windows of opportunity (5.5 Focused Power).

6. *We cannot act now if we are constantly executing plans or distracted by new events*. We don't work on our opportunities because we get locked into plans and because we are distracted by events that have nothing to do with our goals. We do what we had planned to do instead of what we should be doing. Instead of focusing on simple actions to explore simple opportunities, we diffuse our efforts in dozens of different directions (5.2.1 Choosing Adaptability).

7. *In delaying action, even for a day or an hour, windows of opportunities will close.* Conditions will change. Others will take advantages before we do, closing the opening. Our information gets outdated (5.3.2 Opportunity Windows).

8. *Given the proper ingredients for action, acting now will be successful more often than delay*. We must practice to improve our reaction time. If we do develop a prejudice for action, we will develop a reputation for speed and quickness. We will impress our supporters and discourage our adversaries (5.3 Reaction Time).

Illustration:

Let us use an illustration from an area we don't often address, the strategy of making a purchase in a hot market, in this example, purchasing a new house in the hot retail market of a decade ago. This illustration comes from a real-life mistake.

1. *We must develop a prejudice toward taking immediate action to explore opportunities*. If after exploring the market, we find a house that meets our complex criteria at a great price, we must buy it, even if it isn't perfect.

2. *We must internalize the mental models for choosing opportunities and actions.* We will know the right house when we see it. We will feel it in our gut. We must not let our conscious mind's reasonable doubts prevent us from acting when time is critical.

3. As long as an action does not damage our existing position, we should try it. Any house that seems like a great deal will almost certainly be better than our current house.

4. A single action will not likely make a difference, but a pattern of action will. After rejecting a very good house at a great opportunity, we will likely reject future houses because they are not as good.

5. Choosing small actions make acting now much easier. Though there is not small action in buying a house, it starts with simply signing an agreement and risking a deposit.

6. We cannot act now if we are constantly executing plans or distracted by new events. We may have planned to look at twenty different houses before making a purchase, but if we find the right house within the first five, we have a problem. In our case, the third house was the best that we have found in all the years of looking since.

7. In delaying action, even for a day or an hour, windows of opportunities will close. If we wait, maybe even for a day, a good house at a great price will certainly be sold.

8. Given the proper ingredients for action, acting now will be successful more often than delay. We still live in the same house that we bought twenty-five years ago because we didn't act immediately when we found a great house to move to fifteen years ago.

Glossary of Key Concepts from
Sun Tzu's *The Art of War*

This glossary is keyed to the most common English words used in the translation of *The Art of War*. Those terms only capture the strategic concepts generally. Though translated as English nouns, verbs, adverbs, or adjectives, the Chinese characters on which they are based are totally conceptual, not parts of speech. For example, the character for conflict is translated as the noun "conflict," as the verb "fight," and as the adjective "disputed." Ancient written Chinese was a conceptual language, not a spoken one. More like mathematical terms, these concepts are primarily defined by the strict structure of their relationships with other concepts. The Chinese names shown in parentheses with the characters are primarily based on Pinyin, but we occasionally use Cantonese terms to make each term unique.

Advance (*Jeun* 進): to move into new **ground**; to expand your **position**; to move forward in a campaign; the opposite of **flee**.

Advantage, *benefit* (*Li* 利)**:** an opportunity arising from having a better **position** relative to an **enemy**; an opening left by an **enemy**; a **strength** that matches against an **enemy's weakness**; where fullness meets emptiness; a desirable characteristic of a strategic **position**.

Aim, *vision, foresee* (*Jian* 見)**:** **focus** on a specific **advantage**, opening, or opportunity; predicting movements of an **enemy**; a skill of a **leader** in observing **climate**.

Analysis, *plan* (*Gai* 計): a comparison of relative **position**; the examination of the five factors that define a strategic **position**; a combination of **knowledge** and **vision**; the ability to see through **deception**.

Army: see **war.**

Attack, *invade* (*Gong* 攻): a movement to new **ground**; advancing a strategic **position**; action against an **enemy** in the sense of moving into his **ground**; opposite of **defend**; does not necessarily mean **conflict**.

Bad, *ruined* (*Pi* 圮): a condition of the **ground** that makes **advance** difficult; destroyed; terrain that is broken and difficult to traverse; one of the nine situations or types of terrain.

Barricaded: see **obstacles.**

Battle (*Zhan* 戰): to challenge; to engage an **enemy; generically, to meet a challenge; to choose a confrontation with an **enemy** at a specific time and place; to focus all your resources on a task; to establish superiority in a **position**; to challenge an **enemy** to increase **chaos**; that which is **controlled** by **surprise**; one of the four forms of **attack;** the response to a **desperate situation;** character meaning was originally "big meeting," though later took on the meaning "big weapon"; not necessarily conflict.

Bravery, *courage* (*Yong* 勇): the ability to face difficult choices; the character quality that deals with the changes of **CLIMATE;** courage of conviction; willingness to act on vision; one of the six characteristics of a leader.

Break, *broken, divided* (*Po* 破): to **divide** what is **complete**; the absence of a **uniting philosophy**; the opposite of unity.

Calculate, *count* (*Shu* 數): mathematical comparison of quantities and qualities; a measurement of **distance** or troop size.

Change, *transform* (*Bian* 變): transition from one **condition** to another; the ability to adapt to different situations; a natural characteristic of **climate**.

Chaos, *disorder* (*Juan* 亂): **conditions** that cannot be **foreseen**; the natural state of confusion arising from **battle**; one of six weaknesses of an organization; the opposite of **control**.

Claim, *position, form* (*Xing* 形): to use the **ground**; a shape or specific condition of **ground**; the **ground** that you **control**; to use the benefits of the **ground**; the formations of troops; one of the four key skills in making progress.

Climate, *heaven* (*Tian* 天): the passage of time; the realm of uncontrollable **change**; divine providence; the weather; trends that **change** over time; generally, the future; what one must **aim** at in the future; one of five key factors in **analysis;** the opposite of **ground**.

Command (*Ling* 令): to order or the act of ordering subordinates; the decisions of a **leader**; the creation of **methods**.

Competition: see *war.*

Complete: see *unity.*

Condition: see ground.

Confined, *surround* (*Wei* 圍): to encircle; a **situation** or **stage** in which your options are limited; the proper tactic for dealing with an **enemy** that is ten times smaller; to seal off a smaller **enemy**; the characteristic of a **stage** in which a larger **force** can be attacked by a smaller one; one of nine **situations** or **stages**.

Conflict, *fight* (*Zheng* 争): to contend; to dispute; direct confrontation of arms with an **enemy**; highly desirable **ground** that creates disputes; one of nine types of **ground,** terrain, or stages.

Constricted, *narrow* (*Ai* 狹): a confined space or niche; one of six field positions; the limited extreme of the dimension distance; the opposite of **spread-out**.

Control, *govern* (*Chi* 治): to manage situations; to overcome disorder; the opposite of **chaos**.

Dangerous: see **serious.**

Dangers, *adverse* (Ak 阨): a condition that makes it difficult to **advance**; one of three dimensions used to evaluate advantages; the dimension with the extreme field **positions** of **entangling** and **supporting**.

Death, *desperate* (Si 死): to end or the end of life or efforts; an extreme situation in which the only option is **battle**; one of nine **stages** or types of **terrain**; one of five types of **spies**; opposite of **survive**.

Deception, *bluffing, illusion* (Gui 詭): to control perceptions; to control information; to mislead an **enemy**; an attack on an opponent's **aim**; the characteristic of war that confuses perceptions.

Defend (Shou 守): to guard or to hold a **ground**; to remain in a **position**; the opposite of **attack**.

Detour (Yu 迂): the indirect or unsuspected path to a **position**; the more difficult path to **advantage**; the route that is not **direct**.

Direct, *straight* (Jik 直): a straight or obvious path to a goal; opposite of **detour**.

Distance, *distant* (Yuan 遠): the space separating **ground**; to be remote from the current location; to occupy **positions** that are not close to one another; one of six field positions; one of the three dimensions for evaluating opportunities; the emptiness of space.

Divide, *separate* (Fen 分): to break apart a larger force; to separate from a larger group; the opposite of **join** and **focus**.

Double agent, *reverse* (Fan 反): to turn around in direction; to change a situation; to switch a person's allegiance; one of five types of spies.

Easy, *light* (Qing 輕): to require little effort; a **situation** that requires little effort; one of nine **stages** or types of terrain; opposite of **serious**.

Emotion, *feeling* (Xin 心): an unthinking reaction to **aim**, a necessary element to inspire **moves**; a component of esprit de corps; never a sufficient cause for **attack**.

Enemy, *competitor* (Dik 敵): one who makes the same **claim**; one with a similar **goal;** one with whom comparisons of capabilities are made.

Entangling, *hanging* (Gua 懸): a **position** that cannot be returned to; any **condition** that leaves no easy place to go; one of six field positions.

Evade, *avoid* (Bi 避): the tactic used by small competitors when facing large opponents.

Fall apart, *collapse* (Beng 崩): to fail to execute good decisions; to fail to use a **constricted position**; one of six weaknesses of an organization.

Fall down, *sink* (Haam 陷): to fail to make good decisions; to **move** from a **supporting position**; one of six weaknesses of organizations.

Feelings, *affection, love* (_Ching_ 情): the bonds of relationship; the result of a shared **philosophy**; requires management.

Fight, *struggle* (Dou 鬥): to engage in **conflict**; to face difficulties.

Fire (_Huo_ 火): an environmental weapon; a universal analogy for all weapons.

Flee, *retreat, northward* (_Bei_ 北): to abandon a **position**; to surrender **ground**; one of six weaknesses of an **army**; opposite of **advance**.

Focus, *concentrate* (_Zhuan_ 專): to bring resources together at a given time; to **unite** forces for a purpose; an attribute of having a shared **philosophy**; the opposite of *divide*.

Force (_Lei_ 力): power in the simplest sense; a **group** of people bound by **unity** and **focus**; the relative balance of **strength** in opposition to **weakness**.

Foresee: see **aim**.

Fullness: see **strength**.

General: see **leader**.

Goal: see **philosophy**.

Ground, *situation, stage* (_Di_ 地): the earth; a specific place; a specific condition; the place one competes; the prize of competition; one of five key factors in competitive analysis; the opposite of **climate**.

Groups, *troops* (_Dui_ 隊): a number of people united under a shared **philosophy**; human resources of an organization; one of the five targets of fire attacks.

Inside, *internal* (_Nei_ 內): within a **territory** or organization; an insider; one of five types of spies; opposite of _Wai_, outside.

Intersecting, *highway* (_Qu_ 衢): a **situation** or **ground** that allows you to **join**; one of nine types of terrain.

Join (_Hap_ 合): to unite; to make allies; to create a larger **force**; opposite of **divide**.

Knowledge, *listening* (_Zhi_: 知): to have information; the result of listening; the first step in advancing a **position**; the basis of strategy.

Lax, *loosen* (_Shii_ 弛): too easygoing; lacking discipline; one of six weaknesses of an army.

Leader, *general, commander* (_Jiang_ 將): the decision-maker in a competitive unit; one who **listens** and **aims**; one who manages **troops**; superior of officers and men; one of the five key factors in analysis; the conceptual opposite of _fa_, the established methods, which do not require decisions.

Learn, *compare* (_Xiao_ 效): to evaluate the relative qualities of **enemies**.

Listen, *obey* (_Ting_ 聽): to gather **knowledge**; part of **analysis**.

Listening: see **knowledge**.

Local, *countryside* (*Xiang* 鄉): the nearby **ground**; to have **knowledge** of a specific **ground**; one of five types of **spies**.

Marsh (*Ze* 澤): **ground** where footing is unstable; one of the four types of **ground**; analogy for uncertain situations.

Method: see **system**.

Mission: see **philosophy**.

Momentum, *influence* (*Shi* 勢): the **force** created by **surprise** set up by **standards;** used with **timing**.

Mountains, *hill, peak* (*Shan* 山):uneven **ground**; one of four types of **ground**; an analogy for all unequal **situations**.

Move, *march, act* (*Hang* 行): action toward a position or goal; used as a near synonym for <u>dong</u>, act.

Nation (*Guo* 國): the state; the productive part of an organization; the seat of political power; the entity that controls an **army** or competitive part of the organization.

Obstacles, *barricaded* (*Xian* 險): to have barriers; one of the three characteristics of the **ground**; one of six field positions; as a field position, opposite of **unobstructed**.

Open, *meeting, crossing* (*Jiao* 來): to share the same **ground** without conflict; to come together; a **situation** that encourages a race; one of nine **terrains** or **stages**.

Opportunity: see <u>*advantage.*</u>

Outmaneuver (*Sou* 走): to go astray; to be **forced** into a **weak position**; one of six weaknesses of an army.

Outside, *external* (*Wai* 外): not within a **territory** or **army**; one who has a different perspective; one who offers an objective view; opposite of **internal**.

Philosophy, *mission, goals* (*Tao* 道): the shared **goals** that **unite** an **army**; a system of thought; a shared viewpoint; literally "the way"; a way to work together; one of the five key factors in **analysis**.

Plateau (*Liu* 陸): a type of **ground** without defects; an analogy for any equal, solid, and certain **situation**; the best place for competition; one of the four types of **ground**.

Resources, *provisions* (*Liang* 糧): necessary supplies, most commonly food; one of the five targets of fire attacks.

Restraint: see **timing.**

Reward, *treasure, money* (_Bao_ 賞): profit; wealth; the necessary compensation for competition; a necessary ingredient for **victory**; **victory** must pay.

Scatter, *dissipating* (_San_ 散): to disperse; to lose **unity**; the pursuit of separate **goals** as opposed to a central **mission**; a situation that causes a **force** to scatter; one of nine conditions or types of terrain.

Serious, *heavy* (_Chong_ 重): any task requiring effort and skill; a **situation** where resources are running low when you are deeply committed to a campaign or heavily invested in a project; a situation where opposition within an organization mounts; one of nine **stages** or types of **terrain.**

Siege (_Gong Cheng_ 攻城): to move against entrenched positions; any movement against an **enemy's strength**; literally "strike city"; one of the four forms of attack; the least desirable form of attack.

Situation: see **ground.**

Speed, *hurry* (Sai 馳): to **move** over **ground** quickly; the ability to **advance positions** in a minimum of time; needed to take advantage of a window of opportunity.

Spread-out, *wide* (_Guang_ 廣): a surplus of **distance**; one of the six **ground positions**; opposite of **constricted.**

Spy, *conduit, go-between* (_Gaan_ 間): a source of information; a channel of communication; literally, an "opening between."

Stage: see **ground.**

Standard, *proper, correct* (_Jang_ 正): the expected behavior; the standard approach; proven methods; the opposite of surprise; together with **surprise** creates **momentum**.

Storehouse, *house* (_Ku_ 庫): a place where resources are stockpiled; one of the five targets for fire attacks.

Stores, *accumulate, savings* (_Ji_ 糧):resources that have been stored; any type of inventory; one of the five targets of fire attacks.

Strength, *fullness, satisfaction* (_Sat_ 壹): wealth or abundance or resources; the state of being crowded; the opposite of Xu, empty.

Supply wagons, *transport* (_Zi_ 輜): the movement of **resources** through **distance**; one of the five targets of fire attacks.

Support, *supporting* (_Zhii_ 支): to prop up; to enhance; a **ground position** that you cannot leave without losing **strength**; one of six field positions; the opposite extreme of gua, entangling.

Surprise, *unusual, strange* (*Qi* 奇) : the unexpected; the innovative; the opposite of **standard**; together with **standards** creates **momentum**.

Surround: see **confined**.

Survive, *live, birth* (*Shaang* 生): the state of being created, started, or beginning; the state of living or surviving; a temporary condition of fullness; one of five types of spies; the opposite of **death**.

System, *method* (*Fa* 法): a set of procedures; a group of techniques; steps to accomplish a **goal**; one of the five key factors in analysis; the realm of groups who must follow procedures; the opposite of the **leader**.

Territory, *terrain*: see **ground**.

Timing, *restraint* (*Jie* 節): to withhold action until the proper time; to release tension; a companion concept to **momentum**.

Troops: see **group**.

Unity, *whole, oneness* (*Yi* 一): the characteristic of a **group** that shares a **philosophy**; the lowest number; a **group** that acts as a unit; the opposite of **divided**.

Unobstructed, *expert* (*Tong* 通): without obstacles or barriers; **ground** that allows easy movement; open to new ideas; one of six field positions; opposite of **obstructed**.

Victory, *win, winning* (*Sing* 勝): success in an endeavor; getting a reward; serving your mission; an event that produces more than it consumes; to make a profit.

War, *competition, army* (**Bing** 兵): a dynamic situation in which **positions** can be won or lost; a contest in which a **reward** can be won; the conditions under which the principles of strategy work.

Water, *river* (*Shui* 水): a fast-changing **ground**; fluid **conditions**; one of four types of **ground**; an analogy for change.

Weakness, *emptiness, need* (*Xu* 虛): the absence of people or resources; devoid of **force**; the point of **attack** for an **advantage**; a characteristic of **ground** that enables **speed**; poor; the opposite of strength.

Win, *winning*: see **victory**.

Wind, *fashion, custom* (*Feng* 風): the pressure of environmental forces.

The *Art of War Playbook* Series

There are over two-hundred and thirty articles on Sun Tzu's competitive principles in the nine volumes of the *Art of War Playbook*. Each volume covers a specific area of Sun Tzu strategy.

About the Translator and Author

Gary Gagliardi is recognized as America's leading expert on Sun Tzu's *The Art of War*. An award-winning author and business strategist, his many books on Sun Tzu's strategy have been translated around the world. He has appeared on hundreds of talk shows nationwide, providing strategic insight on the breaking news. He has trained decision makers from some of the world's most successful organizations in competitive thinking. His workshops convert Sun Tzu's many principles into a series of practical tools for handling common competitive challenges.

Gary began using Sun Tzu's competitive principles in a successful corporate career and when he started his own software company. In 1990, he wrote his first *Art of War* adaptation for his company's salespeople. By 1992, his company was on *Inc. Magazine's* list of the 500 fastest-growing privately held companies in America. He personally won the U.S. Chamber of Commerce Blue Chip Quality Award and was an Ernst and Young Entrepreneur of the Year finalist. His customers—AT&T, GE, and Motorola, among others—began inviting him to speak at their conferences. After becoming a multimillionaire when he sold his software company in 1997, he continued teaching *The Art of War* around the world.

Gary has authored several breakthrough works on *The Art of War*. Ten of his books on strategy have won book award recognition in nine different non-fiction categories.

Other *Art of War* Books
by Gary Gagliardi

Gary Gagliardi's Books are Available at:

SunTzus.com
Amazon.com
BarnesAndNoble.com
Itunes.apple.com

www.ingramcontent.com/pod-product-compliance
Lightning Source LLC
Chambersburg PA
CBHW062020200326
41519CB00017B/4856